COMMUNITY WORK IN THE 1990s

COMMUNITY WORK
IN THE 1990s

Edited by
Sidney Jacobs
&
Keith Popple

SPOKESMAN

First published in Great Britain in 1994 by
Spokesman
Bertrand Russell House
Gamble Street
Nottingham, England
Tel. 0602 708318
Fax 0602 420433

British Library Cataloguing in Publication Data available on request.
ISBN 0-85124-569-2 paper ✓

Printed by the Russell Press Ltd, Nottingham
(Tel. 0115 9784505)

Dedicated to the memory of Phil Bashford
(1947-1986)
An inspirational community worker, teacher
and dear friend

Contents

Introduction

Community work in the 1990s, having survived the battering of the Thatcher years, needs to recapture its radical traditions. Community work's survival during the 1980s demanded considerable flexibility and innovation, which is reflected in a diversity of initiatives spread throughout the country. Some of these are presented here. This book was conceived by friends of Phil Bashford because we believe that it is important to affirm the values that he represented within community work with which, through untiring example, he influenced so many of us. His was essentially a humane response to society's ills and his vision was of a collectivist and democratic future. He passionately believed in the ability of the exploited and oppressed everywhere to organise themselves under their own leadership against injustice. It is these principles that this book hopes to keep alive within community work.

Paul Waddington begins the volume with a chapter that places values at the heart of the community work enterprise. He believes that one of the central values that unites practitioners is the desire to promote 'civic virtue' and create a democracy of free and equal citizens. Bob Holman, adopting an historical perspective, takes up a similar theme arguing that socialist values need to be at the centre of both the theory and practice of community work; and that means promoting socialism in our everyday lives. Keith Popple's chapter, which follows, highlights the possibilities of developing a progressive community work praxis that utilises the work of Antonio Gramsci and Paulo Friere.

Ranjit Sondhi, in a wide-ranging discussion of racism, examines the implications for Britain's black community of the single European Market after 1992. Lena Dominelli then focuses on the centrality of feminist theory and practice to community work. In the following chapter, Viv Rogers analyses her work as a community education tutor in Plymouth on a women-only course. The chapter by Nick Derricourt and Jen Dale provides a case study of community work practice in Rochdale which focuses on alliance making. Haydae White, in her paper, draws upon her experiences of organising support and training for black workers in Bristol. George Giarchi then argues the case for rural community work. Ann Jeffries provides an overview and critical assessment of community organising in the United States, demonstrating the lessons to be learnt from the U.S. experience. In the following chapter, Martin Wood discusses the idea of radical community work as applied to the struggles of council house tenants. Finally, Sid Jacobs examines the role of community work following the collapse of communism. He suggests that its primary function, now purely defensive, is to attempt to organise among the growing numbers in poverty at the bottom of society.

We would like to thank all those who encouraged us to produce this volume and who never lost faith that eventually we would succeed. We are heavily indebted to the untiring work of the secretaries in the Department of Applied Social Science at the University of Plymouth, in particular Sue Ellicott and Margaret Holwell. We would also like to thank Spokesman Books and in particular Tony Simpson for his patience and support in seeing this publication into print.

Finally, we wish this book to stand as a tribute to Liz Bashford and the children, Tina, Sonia, Nicholas, Katherine, Joe and Stephen.

Sid Jacobs
Keith Popple
May 1994

The Values Base of Community Work

Paul Waddington

This chapter is based on the second Phil Bashford Annual Memorial Lecture which I had the privilege of delivering to a mixed audience comprising Phil's family and friends, professionals and community activists, academics and students at Plymouth in February 1989.

As a friend and former teaching and professional colleague of Phil's, I chose a topic which would enable me to express the way in which my life had been touched by his. Like many others, I was profoundly moved by Phil Bashford's early death and, as is the way with such experiences, it caused me to reflect on the direction of my own life.

It was within this context and for this mixed audience that I put the emphasis of the paper on the centrality of values in the community work enterprise and on how they should condition what we actually do.

To write about values, ultimate purpose and moral principles is not an easy task in a field like community work, or any other area of practical activity for that matter. To a sophisticated audience the topic may smack of sentimentality or of exposure to moral rearmament. However, my inclination to see the topic of values re-enthroned at the heart of the community work enterprise has received encouragement from the fact that some of those involved in the reconstruction of socialist strategy are now engaged in a debate in which similar concerns have become central.

The Question of Values and Purpose in Community Work

There is not, in my experience, a great deal of contemporary discussion about values amongst community workers and the topic does not figure very largely in the recent literature of the subject, at least in explicit form.

There has been a good deal of writing about what community workers need to be able to do and about the skills and attributes required for effective performance of the task. These more technical or professional aspects of the job have always had a higher profile in the American literature on the subject of community organisation, reflecting amongst other factors the very different cultural traditions and organisational characteristics of that country. Within this general framework the emphasis is placed on the worker's needs for skills in situational analysis, problem-solving, organisation building and maintenance, communication and interaction with people, groupwork, programme development etc. Henderson and Thomas (1987) have sought to adapt and develop this kind of more technical thinking about the task in Britain and their articulation of community work as an orderly and reflective process has been an influential contribution.

There has also been a very different tradition of writing about community work which has been more explicitly concerned to politically link organisational activities at neighbourhood level and local campaigns around issues with more broadly-based movements for social reform. Within this tradition, the emphasis is placed on the worker's needs for an adequate structural/materialist analysis within which to identify and foster localised points of struggle around substantive issues where the potential exists for raising consciousness and making broader political connections.

Whilst I have observed the high degree of professional, and sometimes personal, antipathy shown by proponents of each school of thought to those of the other tendency over the years, my own view is that the community work enterprise needs to seek to combine the perspectives and attributes of both. It can only do so, however, and then imperfectly, within a framework of thinking about practice which honestly recognises the uncertainties involved in the inevitably muddled and chaotic world of day to day practice at neighbourhood level. It is in this context that the values which inform the practice of community workers are so important and require more explicit recognition and more open sharing in professional discussions than they have been given in recent years. In neither of the schools of thought, the technical and the materialist, are underlying values given much serious attention. This leaves open to question why community workers actually spend their lives doing what they do.

Like all of us, Phil Bashford was a complex person with his own contradictions. However, an important element of his approach to the practice of community work was his determination to keep things as simple as possible, thus allowing full scope for the use of an informed intuition in what is inevitably an artistic rather than a scientific activity.

Reduced to its essentials, I think that his view of our business was as follows. Firstly that the heart of community work is in practice at the grassroots. Of course such practice is informed by the participants' values and by their political/ideological perspectives, and it needs to be engaged in reflectively. But by its nature and uncertain day to day operation, practice is always organic and can never creatively fit within a slavishly applied theory, model or 'correct position'. Rightly, he was intolerant of that absolute reductionism inherent in all intellectual, academic and ideological activity insofar as it tends to foreclose on what is possible in the future from a position of abstract speculation. Gramsci's maxim in this connection was "pessimism of the intellect, optimism of the will".

Secondly, that community work is essentially about the experience of personal liberation through collective activity of all those who participate in it. But its particular mission is with the empowerment of dispossessed and excluded groups — the working class, women, black people, older people and the disabled. It follows, therefore, that community workers have to take sides and be partisan.

Thirdly — and perhaps most importantly — community work is a moral activity, involving moral actors, striving for moral ends or goals and with a practice which should embody the attempt to apply moral principles. In this context it matters a great deal that community workers are seen to be making earnest attempts to practice what they preach and to achieve an appropriate fit between their personal and their political attitudes and behaviour.[1] Put very simply, what unites all of us who are involved in community work is a commitment to the achievement of a dream. It is the idea that through the sharing of experience, the process of learning through action, the attempt to grapple with problems and meet needs (albeit that they may sometimes be beyond our reach) and via collective and democratic processes of organisation at neighbourhood level, we can better realise our potential as human beings and contribute to the creation of a better and fairer world.

Inextricably mixed up in this enterprise are notions of personal growth and encounter; promotion of neighbourhood identity, caring and health; self help; and political organising and struggle. Inevitably, different individuals and groups involved in community work will put the emphasis on different aspects according to personal and political attitudes or local and practical circumstances. It is also important to note that different actors in the theatre of community work will define notions like 'social justice', 'equality' and 'freedom' in different ways and will identify different practical and political routes towards their achievement.

The Contemporary Context

Having observed earlier that any attempt to engage in discussion of values in community work is fraught with difficulties and moral ambiguities, it seems worthwhile to identify some of the reasons why this is so and why, paradoxically, it is timely for us to again make that attempt.

One reason is that community work has been engaged in a long struggle to escape from its origins in charitable work, including the activities of churches, the ethos of 'the voluntary sector', the contribution of professionals and missionaries returning to this country with the collapse of empire, etc. There has also been a very strong gut-felt need to establish a clear-cut separation from social work with its perceived association with psycho-analytical and personal inadequacy explanations and solutions for social problems. As community workers have struggled up the long hill towards recognition of occupational identity and, perhaps, professional status and as the times have changed through the 1970s, 1980s, and 1990s we have developed a tougher style of discourse in which words like 'issues', 'campaigns', 'strategies', 'skills', 'resources' have replaced an earlier and more value-laden currency.

In many ways, of course, this is a product of the times we live in. Late twentieth century society is firmly secular and materialist in nature. Organised religion and morally-based institutions and frameworks of thinking have much less influence now on political life and policy-making. The processes of secularisation, centralisation and cultural disintegration, and the modern world's and state's demand for technical knowledge and pragmatic instrumentality have made us all distrustful of moral knowledge and uneasy with moral questions, even though moral exhortations remain politically useful tools. This distrust and unease have been reflected in the recent discourse and literature of community work.

However, an important aspect of the success of the Conservative Government arose from the way in which over the last decade or so it not only seized on moral political discourse but also reversed its basis and assumed the high moral ground. 'Enterprise' replaced 'greed' in the political lexicon and the cultivation of 'national unity' has disguised the active reinforcement of social divisions. The vigorous promotion of a particular version of the idea of 'freedom' was used in the attempt to remove 'equality', 'compassion' and 'redistributive social justice' from the political agenda. The incorporation of more and more areas of what used to be called 'civil society' within the ambit of state power substantially diminished civil liberties.

Quite obviously, this represented not only a very direct onslaught on the values and policies which underpinned the Conservative Government's explicitly declared enemy, Socialism, but also the post-war consensus and basis for the establishment of the Welfare State. It savaged the life chances and opportunities for effective political participation of most of the social groups and neighbourhoods with which the overwhelming majority of community workers are engaged and effectively denied the values base for the activity of community workers, except in the most residual terms.

In this context, a degree of *'de-moralisation'* amongst community workers is inevitable. One response, especially given the ongoing problems of securing continued funding, is to retreat from paid fieldwork (as it will be noted, the author did some time ago). Another is to demonstrate enterprise by seeking to capitalise on the opportunities for community work entrepreneurship and funding which have emerged in the new scheme of things. Yet another response, and a very worthy one, is to battle on stoically and hope for better days. The nature of fieldwork in any case is that there is neither much time nor opportunity to engage in a great deal of reflection and especially on more philosophical issues which do not appear to engender much hope of quick or practically effective resolution.

It is my experience that everyone needs to feel that what they are doing is worthwhile and to know, however intuitively, why they are doing it. This is particularly essential if what they are doing is something as stressful and full of uncertainty and ambiguity as community work. Given the nature of the task and the political context in which it now has to be done, it is not surprising that the rate of occupational turnover and drop-out is so high. It would hardly be possible to persuade a substantial and growing cadre of experienced workers to remain in the job for the money and career prospects presently available alone!

Paradoxically, it is at times of greatest social change, uncertainty and 'paradigmatic shift' that a capacity to mentally retreat somewhat from an endless series of tasks and into a process of reflective taking stock is most essential. As writers like Bettelheim (1961) have shown, to maintain hope in an alien environment, we have to develop our capacity for inventing and re-inventing, believing in and communicating to others, alternative visions of how things could be and for pointing to some credible initial steps along the way. To do this means going back to, and reconsidering, first principles and values. We may have to be content at this stage with a language of visions and elemental schemata, since grand strategies and plans may be currently beyond us.

It would be an error to lay the necessity for intellectual reconstruction, not only of activities like community work but also of left politics, entirely at the door of the Conservative Government. In a wider sense, it is the predicament of Post-Modern Woman/Man to have to learn to live within a world of ultimate uncertainty, absolute relativism of values and underlying ontological terror. Mrs Thatcher's was one way forward: it assumed that all that remains is ego and the will to power and domination and that the motor of social life has to be the cultivation of a rampant individualism. It is ironic, given our retreat from the origins of community work, that along with others we will have to develop further our ability to perform effectively as a kind of 'secular priesthood' if we are to contribute to the future realisation of an alternative vision. In this connection, however, I would remind you of an exchange near the end of Becket's "Waiting for Godot":-

"I can't go on like this."

"That's what you think."

After a period of profound social and political crisis, disarray and pessimism (at least to the left of the far right), community workers can draw comfort and derive inspiration and ideas from the evidence of fresh thinking on the left and in related academic circles, as well as from indicators of electoral preferences. The vigorous discussions in the columns of journals like the *New Statesman and Society* and the now defunct *Marxism Today* and elsewhere have suggested that the challenge to the left is to respond to what are referred to as the 'New Times' or 'Post-Fordism'. Risking over-simplification, the analysis suggests that this is a period when modern industrial societies are being fundamentally re-shaped, after a period of stagnation and structural crisis in the 1970s. This reshaping process involves the disintegration of the old order of society and with it the continuity of social life and class allegiances etc. The introduction of constant change with its destabilising consequences is both an inevitable outcome as well as an intended effect of government policy. There is no possibility of going back to the old order or the old post-war policy.

These analysts suggest that the Thatcher Government had recognised this new economic and social terrain and sought to make it their own via an equally fundamental restructuring of political forces, whilst most of the left, caught up with old allegiances, has struggled to make a similar adjustment. This it must now do and the evidence suggests that the process of intellectual reconstruction is underway. Apart from noting that we can now add 'Post-Fordism' and 'Post-Modernism' to Daniel Bell's (1974) twenty-odd 'Post-Something or Others', it is not my intention to attempt to further develop this discussion of the debate about 'New Times' here. The point is that the challenge of profound change to, and the need for intellectual reconstruction of, the community work enterprise is part of a much wider process affecting society.

The Debate About Citizenship

As part of this intellectual reconstruction work on the left, the debate about citizenship has been particularly apposite and timely for those engaged in community work.

Speeches by Ministers, together with the logic of government policy across the board in areas like health, housing, education, social security, local government responsibilities etc indicate that it is the government's intention that the state should progressively abdicate from many of its present responsibilities, except in the most marginal and residual terms. The responsibility for social provision is to be 'privatised'. But to whom, and wherein in this lie social obligation and the notion of citizenship?

The disturbed public and political reaction to Mrs Thatcher's unwise statement that there is no such thing as society, only a collection of individuals and the family, was followed by the hurried discovery by Douglas Hurd, when Home Secretary, and by other Conservative 'wets' of the hitherto forgotten or unnoticed virtues of 'the active citizen' (ie the great army of unpaid people queuing up to join the community groups we work with). It is the task of these active citizens, women especially no doubt, to pick up the tab of meeting needs for which the public sector relinquishes responsibility. The question of where the resources will come from has not been addressed. As David Marquand (1980) put it, the closure of traditional institutions and introduction of community care policy means that the care of the mentally ill and handicapped and of the elderly is farmed out to an abstraction called the community. So much for equal opportunity for women!

The notion of 'citizenship' is now back on the political agenda, although it will be interesting to see how long it remains there given that a short while ago it seemed to be regarded as a rather archaic political concept. There have been a number of contributions to the debate of which Raymond Plant's (1988) Fabian Society Pamphlet will be of particular interest to community work readers.

Plant suggests that within the reconstruction of political thinking by the New Right, and with some lag, on the left, the principal distinction between the two competing political philosophies so far as the definition of citizenship is concerned lies in breadth of compass. For the New Right, the role of the state should be restricted to providing a framework of laws which seeks only to prevent coercion of one individual by another. The notion of citizenship, according to this view, has nothing whatsoever to do with an individual's ability to achieve wants and therefore with concepts of redistributive justice or achievement of fair allocation of resources by political action or state policy. Poverty is not unfreedom, according to Sir Keith Joseph. It is argued that not only would a programme of political action for redistribution not achieve the desired outcome practically; it would not be 'moral' to attempt to do so since social justice (the central tenet of socialism) has no moral basis.

This has been strongly countered from the left, by Plant and others like Marquand, with the view that a version of freedom and therefore citizenship which confines itself to a residual legal framework and completely disregards questions related to the relative ability, power and resources of its different citizens and social groups (ie with 'agency') and to the interventive role of the state, is a completely inadequate one for any modern industrial society which puts any premium whatsoever on fairness — and ultimately, it might be added, on social cohesion and stability. Implicit in such an approach to citizenship has to be acceptance of some reduction in individual liberty. It is acknowledged by Plant that one of the central dilemmas for socialist reconstruction lies in achieving an appropriate rebalancing of the individualist (freedom) and the collectivist (equality, social justice) impulses of socialism.

David Marquand (1988) has made the telling point that by a crucial, and presumably unconscious, irony the current version of conservative thinking on 'the active citizen' (after Hurd *et al*) is the very antithesis of the real thing. The very notion of citizen implies the *polis*, the city, the community, the collective realm, where the performance of obligations, both 'private' and 'public', derives from participation in a political community. It is a two-way relationship and the concept of citizenship has an inextricable connection with the notion of democracy.

Conclusion
The renewed interest in national political debate about the concept of citizenship from both ends of the political spectrum suggests that there is more than a little mileage left in community work. The connection between the underlying purpose and values of

community work and the promotion and achievement of citizenship is obvious.

It is very clear today — as it has been throughout recent history — that both wings of political opinion and future governments of whatever kind will continue to seek to appropriate to themselves notions like 'community' and 'citizenship'. Either way it seems likely that we shall be required to stay in business, although the imperatives for analysis and successful organising may be very different ones.

Like many others on the left of the political spectrum, most community workers have become suspicious over the years about invitations to engage in discussion of fundamental values and morality. To do so has tended to be regarded as naive, self-indulgent and politically unrealistic. But times are changing. The achievements of Thatcherism and the new lines of thinking towards an intellectual reconstruction of the Socialist movement point to the need for community workers too to re-engage in debate about fundamentals. Thus might we rediscover why the word 'Fraternity' was included in the Socialist Trinity. More directly than 'Liberty' and 'Equality' it demands a moral quality in our practice. However, since an obvious difficulty with the term 'Fraternity' for contemporary usage arises from its sexism, there is a need to find an alternative — how about 'Community'?

Footnote
1. I have not put any emphasis on the moral mission of community work with the intention of canonising Phil Bashford (who was actually a very earthy and unsanctimonious person) nor have I meant to reduce the essentials of community work to a series of trite cliches. I have done so in an attempt to expose what actually and potentially unites those of us who engage in community work, rather than dwelling on what may analytically and ideologically be seen as dividing us. The congregation of community work is a very broad church indeed.

   I am very aware that a likely response or objection to the formulation above is that it is a hopelessly muddled humanistic/liberal statement which in itself does not necessarily get us anywhere and/or is an insufficient basis for action. It is also necessary for many workers to engage in political analysis — about the role of the state, the structural nature of inequality, the ways in which social divisions are created and reinforced — and to give careful consideration to questions of political strategy.

   Nevertheless, I maintain that it is important to attempt to identify and emphasise that which unites those of us who are involved in community work and that which gives a fundamental and shared purpose to our work. Essentially, our commitment is to a moral enterprise involving people working together at neighbourhood or grassroots level which is concerned with the promotion of the practice of 'civic virtue' and the creation of the fullest possible democracy of free and equal citizens.

   This does seem quite a sizeable aspiration! It is important to recognise that it is beyond the scope of community work in itself — still less its cadre of paid or professional workers — to achieve such an end. It may also be that aspirations expressed so broadly may not ultimately be achievable, certainly not in the short term and short of the millennium, and are in the nature of ever-receding horizons.

References

Bell, D. (1974) *The Coming of Post-Industrial Society*, Heinemann.

Bettelheim, B. (1961) *The Informed Heart*, Thames and Hudson.

Gramsci, A. (1971) in Hoare, Q. and Nowell Smith, G. (Eds) *Selections from the Prison Notebooks of Antonio Gramsci*, Lawrence and Wishart, p.175.

Henderson, P. and Thomas, D.N. (1987) *Skills in Neighbourhood Work*, (2nd edition). Allen and Unwin.

Marquand, D. (1988) *The Unprincipled Society*, Fontana.

Plant, R. (1988) *Citizenship, Rights and Socialism*, Fabian Society Pamphlet No.531.

2

Socialism as Living

Bob Holman*

Community Work is the theme of this volume. Yet when I knew Phil Bashford, he did not regard himself as a community worker. Rather, I think he saw himself as a resident who wanted to help the community in which he lived. He became the assistant leader of a newly formed Adventure Playground in the inner ring area of Handsworth in Birmingham. Despite possessing no formal qualifications in community or social work he became a successful, much liked, even beloved, worker at the Handsworth Adventure Playground. It was a tough job where local youngsters tested him to the full. The playground was run on a shoestring budget. The only shelter on the site was an unheated wooden hut which contained one battered table tennis table. I can still see Phil, clad in an enormous overcoat which he bought at the playground's jumble sale, dealing patiently with the local young people who gathered around him. Somehow, through cold winters and demanding circumstances, he retained that engaging smile, cheerfulness and attitude of encouragement which endeared him to the Handsworth population. Perhaps these qualities also endeared him to Elizabeth Badenoch, whom I had introduced to the playground, for soon they married.

In later years, Phil Bashford was to develop analytical and teaching skills as he became a well known trainer of community workers. Yet, at this early period, it was his personal qualities which served him well at the playground and in the locality and which made such an impression on other people. Of course, the teaching and practice of community work is important. But there is a danger that an undue emphasis on community work — or on any other occupation — can divide life into compartments such as work and leisure, skills and personality, employment and home, clients and

*Bob Holman delivered the first Phil Bashford Memorial Lecture on Community Work, Plymouth Polytechnic (now the University of Plymouth), Plymouth 1988 [see Holman 1988].

friends, which somehow detract from the wholeness of living. This understanding came more fully to me some years after my friendship with Phil when I led a community project based on our home. In that setting it became difficult if not impossible to distinguish between work and non-work.

If a parent knocked on the door on a Saturday afternoon in order to discuss a difficulty, I could not refuse to listen on the grounds that I was not paid to work at weekends. If a youngster dropped in for a game of pool, I did not know whether I was at work in building up a relationship with him or her or whether we were just relaxing at a game we both enjoyed. In short, by having a job based on a family home, there came a wholeness which I had not experienced in previous posts where I had commuted to work. Moreover, the impact of that project, depended not just upon our professional and occupational skills but also upon our personal qualities (or deficiencies) as neighbours, friends and members of the community.

My argument, then, is that the building of better services, communities, even societies, demands more than professional skills. It requires better lives. In his days at Handsworth, Phil Bashford was effective and impressive because he appeared to have a philosophy or set of beliefs which was expressed in his attitudes, actions and behaviour at the adventure playground, at home, and in the neighbourhood. Phil was a socialist and this leads me to the subject of my chapter which is "Socialism as Living". For just as Phil was more than a community worker so I will argue that a socialist is more than a voter, a party member or even an elected representative. This chapter is written not just to honour Phil but rather as a way of offering thanks for his life.

Ethical Socialists
The roots of socialism rest in men and women who were dissatisfied with the world around them and who argued for one based on different values and different practices. One such group of men and women were the Ethical Socialists who had a strong influence in Victorian and Edwardian times. Recently, attention to the Ethical Socialists has been recalled by the writings of Norman Dennis and A.H. Halsey (1988). Like the Marxists, they recognised the extent of and the ill-effects of social class divisions and the need of united working class action to remove them. Unlike the Marxists, they tended to emphasise co-operation and reform rather than violent conflict and revolution — indeed, many were pacifists. Like the Fabians, they believed in constitutional and democratic routes to change. Unlike the Fabians, they distrusted the role of professional

elites and experts. They drew heavily upon Christian Socialists like John Ruskin who spoke about both the dignity of individuals and the need for harmonious communities where all talents contributed to the common good and where goods were distributed according to need.

A leading Ethical Socialist was Edward Carpenter whose *Towards Democracy*, published in 1882, went through several editions. Interestingly, Carpenter's book was not entitled "Towards Socialism", for he never advocated the complete removal of the capitalistic system. But he bitterly criticised the ethics of capitalism with its worship of money and the sacrifice of the health and interests of many working class people for the profits of a minority of owners and managers. He explained vividly how the practice of capitalism damaged the quality of relationships amongst and between all social classes.

John Bruce Glasier, like Keir Hardie and Ramsay MacDonald, was a Scot whose socialism grew out of his understanding of Christianity. His wife, Katherine, became a socialist after seeing ill-fed strikers invade a rich Bristol church. Together they wrote a number of books of which the best known was *The Religion of Socialism*, published in 1890. Again, the title is significant for they regarded socialism as a faith, a kind of religion which could inspire individuals to live by its code of conduct and to sacrifice their money, possessions and even their lives in its furtherance.

Robert Blatchford had a greater impact than either the Glasiers or Carpenter. His importance stemmed from not just what he said, but more on the size and range of his audience. A journalist, he founded a journal, *The Clarion*, which combined articles on socialism with reports on sport and other topical events which soon won it a wide working class readership. In 1894, he published his famous *Merrie England*, written in a straightforward style, which became the most widely read socialist book of the decade. In it — and in his other writings — Blatchford effectively contrasted the riches and poverty, the health and disease, the privileges and deprivations of Britain. In its place, he offered the vision of a new, socialist Britain, free from squalor and distress and with adequate homes, gardens and incomes for all.

The Ethical Socialists had many limitations. The Glasiers failed to perceive that a collective State might be a force for evil as well as good. Blatchford appeared to think that Britain could revert to a yeoman, agrarian society. In general, the Ethical Socialists were accused of being impractical and utopian. Yet, as Geoffrey Foote (1987, p.37) concludes, they made a significant contribution to the growing Labour movement. He states that their "moralistic critique of the corruption and degradation of a competitive society was to be at the heart of British socialism" and in its place they put forward the vision of "an unselfish and caring community (which) would one day replace an indifferent and cruel social order". The Ethical Socialists pleaded for a society whose mainspring would be collective well-being rather than individual gain: in which rewards and responsibilities would be distributed as equally as possible: and in which human relationships would be characterised by harmony not hatred. In broad strokes, they painted a picture of the values which make up socialism.

It is one thing to talk and write about the ethics of socialism, quite another to put them into practice. Yet the history of British socialism is graced by figures who took its values not just as the basis of a utopian future but also as a faith to be expressed in their daily lives. Helena Born, for instance, on becoming a socialist left her affluent Bristol district to reside in down-town St. Philips. There she worked tirelessly, often tramping thirty miles a day, to unionise the home-based and ill-paid seamstresses. Helena Born was a socialist feminist who, unlike some of her contemporaries, was less concerned that privileged, middle class women should obtain the same status and rewards as middle class men, and more concerned that working class women should gain access to political and social life. She endured much hostility, lived simply, and wrote, "The principles of Socialism, as I understand them, seem to me economically incontrovertible, and to comprise spiritual ideals of unity and brotherhood which alone can transmute the materialism of our time. And I feel that the only way to convince others of the truth of one's principles, and to bring about the new time, is by living them . . . It is uphill work but we cannot isolate ourselves from the mass." (*Bristol's Other History*, 1984, p.118).

George Lansbury
Little is now known about the middle class Helena Born. Much more is known about the working class George Lansbury. Pacifists who called for the end of hostilities during the Great War were not generally popular figures. Yet Lansbury could fill the Royal Albert Hall when not only calling for peace but while also welcoming the revolution in Russia. In 1931, the Labour Party was almost wiped out at the polls following the desertion of Ramsay MacDonald and the formation of a national coalition. Lansbury then replaced MacDonald as the Labour leader although he was by then in his seventies and inexperienced in high office. Why did he attract crowds? Why was he chosen as leader? The reasons stem from his personal qualities, because he represented what a socialist should

be. He had resisted numerous financial inducements despite coming from a poor background, having a low income and a large family. His son, Edgar, recalled his father's generosity and told how once he took out a loan, which he could ill-afford, in order to set up a needy friend in a small business (E. Lansbury (1934), p.65). Edgar, himself a Labour councillor, died young of cancer. His death was one of several tragedies borne courageously by Lansbury. As a councillor and then Member of Parliament, Lansbury disliked free meals, free booze and free accommodation at conferences. He reasoned that if ordinary poor people could not have such "freebies" then neither should he. He would not even have a study of his own while others were homeless. He refused to move from Bow to the more comfortable suburbs saying, "I would sooner be here in the Bow Rd where the unemployed can put a brick through my window when they disagree with any activities, than be in some other place far away where they can only write a letter". (Holman, (1990) p.86).

Lansbury was also unusual in insisting that socialism applied to women as well as men. As early as the 1880s, he was campaigning for women's rights. Unlike many campaigners, he insisted that the vote be given to working class and not just middle class women while he also argued that the former were economically as well as politically oppressed. He provoked some well-to-do women to fury by his articles calling for more employment opportunities for women and he was the chair of one of the first organisations to establish day nurseries where the children of working mothers could be cared for in a satisfactory matter. Such was the strength of his feeling that in 1912 he resigned his seat in the Commons when Labour colleagues failed to support him in opposing the government's inadequate suffrage bill. His wife Bessie was the subject of a misjudgement by Sylvia Pankhurst, during her temporary stay in the East End, when she wrote that "Her (Bessie's) exceptionally large family had long debarred her from activity in the Labour movement" (Pankhurst, 1978, p.426-7). Certainly, Bessie had 12 children and was devoted to those who survived. But she also participated in local politics and, during the war-time, was the director of a project to help local families and was also the secretary of the League of Rights for Soldiers' and Sailors' Wives and Relatives. Bessie supported the votes campaign but, as her son Edgar explained, was suspicious of its middle class leadership and ". . . resented their coming into Bow and sidetracking the enthusiasm of the growing movement for Socialism into an agitation for votes for women which in her view was always a subsidiary issue". (E. Lansbury, 1934, p.140). Like George, Bessie Lansbury regarded socialism as something which affected her everyday living and she was determined to maintain her solidarity with other working class women.

George Lansbury, too, refused to be drawn into the middle class establishment. Unlike MacDonald, he spurned both the company of establishment figures and the honours system. "Good, old George", as he became known, was listened to and elected because he was respected and loved. As it happened, he turned out to be a fine leader of the Labour Party and Michael Foot, in describing the heroic re-building of the party after 1931, has stated that Lansbury was the "embodiment" of its "idealism and pragmatism" (Foot, 1987). While leader, and indeed throughout his political life, Lansbury advocated wide-ranging reforms which would have abolished poverty and promoted equality. But he never neglected the role of individuals. Thus he wrote,

> I yield to no one my downright hatred of the present social order, built as it is on fraud and cunning, make-believe and humbug; but I cannot believe in any change being real unless it starts from individual men and women. (Groser 1949, p.24).

To the end, he was an example of an individual who lived socialism. He remained a person of the people with his home always open to those in need. He died, still at 39, Bow Road, almost penniless yet rich in the kind of life he had lived.

The example of the likes of Born and Lansbury was infectious and the Labour Party grew numerically. They won to socialism people like Jim Simmons who became a political force in Birmingham (Simmons 1972). The attraction was not just the promise of an alternative to capitalism in the future but also the demonstration that socialism made better men and women in the present. During this period, socialism was both expounded as a set of principles and practised as a code which guided people in the daily conduct of their private and public affairs.

Today
Today the Labour Party still has leading figures who expound the principles of socialism. Much less in evidence is the personal application. For instance, Roy Hattersley (1987) divides his *Choose Freedom: the Future for Democratic Socialism* into two parts, The Principles and The Practice. In the former, he starts with a chapter on "In Praise of Ideology", writes eloquently about equality and liberty, and accepts the definition of socialism as "the pursuit of equality and the protection of freedom". In the latter, practice is discussed in terms of the relative merits of the competitive market system and state ownership of the means of production rather than

in terms of the individual's practice of socialism. Again, in a Fabian pamphlet Margaret Drabble (1988) has re-stated cogently her belief in equality. However, she gives little consideration as to how socialists — including those who reside in Hampstead — should apply equality to their own lifestyles. Of course, the Labour Party still contains practising socialists. But in terms of public impact they are overshadowed by former radicals whose expressions of solidarity with the socially deprived fade as they climb the social ladder. The practising activists are no longer a national influence. Few books are published on socialism and individual conduct. Party resolutions rarely contain resolutions on the subject.

It is timely, therefore, to re-formulate socialism as a faith which is applied to individual attitudes and actions. A socialist society will be one in which gross inequalities are removed and in which relationships are characterised by fellowship rather than enmity. So I suggest that a socialist life is one which reflects that kind of society in the here and now. I propose three guidelines which can underpin such a life, namely sufficing, vacating and sharing.

Sufficing
If socialists desire a population without great differences of incomes then it is strange that some are prepared to take incomes of £40,000 per annum or more while others receive less than £9,000 (or under £3,000 if in receipt of Income Support). Even within statutory and voluntary welfare agencies, chief executives who profess both to be socialists and to favour equality, have no hesitation in availing themselves of the kind of excessive salaries which reinforce the enormous differentials within the nation. As the Claimants' Unions say, "There's a lot of money to be made out of poverty". I have heard such affluent socialists justify their high incomes on the grounds that they can give more to charities. The Liberal, Sir Samuel Montagu, tried that one on Lansbury saying, "I am a . . . better socialist than you. I give a tenth of my riches each year to the poor." Lansbury replied, "Yes, I know how good you are . . . but we socialists want to prevent you getting the nine tenths. We do not believe in rich and poor and charity." (G. Lansbury, 1928, p.75).

Socialists can display their sincerity by declining high salaries whatever their posts and responsibilities. Their principle should be that of sufficiency, that is an income sufficient for their needs not their luxuries. Personally, I reached the point where I considered it wrong to accept a salary in excess of average earnings. I know a head of one national agency who takes less than that. His motto is need not greed. The money saved by such actions, if distributed, might not of itself eliminate financial inequalities. But the widespread adoption of sufficiency would be a statement that socialists are not prepared to be a part of the mechanisms which uphold poverty and it would be a public indication of their determination to work towards a more equal society.

Vacating

Central to socialism is the notion that positions of leadership and influence should not be dominated by elites but should be open in practice as well as in theory to those from socially disadvantaged backgrounds. Implicit in this aspect of equality is that not only do the latter have the right but also the capacity to occupy such roles. Unfortunately, mechanisms of class, gender and race bar the way. It might be thought that until these barriers are removed, socialists from advantageous circumstances would be prepared voluntarily to cede their posts to others. Sadly, it is not so. Even in Lansbury's day, he observed that outsiders from the "right" kind of schools often exploited poor people by coming to work in the East End of London and then using that experience to obtain top posts for themselves. His view was that middle class socialists of this kind should have striven to enable the East Enders to obtain these positions. Several decades later, the same type of middle class leaders often speak out loudly in favour of equal opportunities in employment yet somehow the top jobs are still dominated by affluent, white people — like themselves. Equality of access for working class women, members of ethnic minorities and those from socially depriving backgrounds applies only to lower grade jobs. To these socialists, equal opportunity is a fine principle provided it does not harm their careers.

An alternative is the practice of vacating whereby the privileged deliberately make way for others. Already examples exist at neighbourhood level where community project leaders have vacated their posts for local residents to take over. Now it needs applying to larger organisations so that people from a wider social range — including those from the inner cities and peripheral housing schemes — can obtain those positions which do so much to determine the distribution of incomes and opportunities in Britain.

Sharing

It is a truism to say that Britain is a divided nation. At one extreme are the top five per cent of income earners who enjoy secure employment in good working conditions, who reside in spacious, private houses, who eat plentifully and dress well, who take holidays abroad and who will retire with comfortable pensions. At the other end are the bottom ten per cent who survive on Income Support or low wages in poor working environments, who dwell in damp or crowded homes, and who eke out old age on a state pension. In Easterhouse, I see daily families who rarely travel outside the estate, whose children miss out on fresh fruit and vegetables, who are prone to ill-health and for whom a holiday is almost unknown. This material divide has led to social and geographical divides so that members of the different sides do not know or relate to each other.

The creed of socialism cannot accept such divisions. It holds that the material goods of the earth are the possession of all and should not be dominated by one group to the exclusion of others. But beyond materialism, it also believes that the very fact of being human ties people together in bonds of mutual responsibility. It follows that individuals can practise socialism by sharing. The deprived can not locate themselves near the privileged. But socialists with the advantage of choice can decide to reside alongside those in greater need than themselves and so be in a position to share their homes, their possessions, their money, their holidays, with those who have less. More, they can share themselves, their emotions, their love, their living. And, in so doing, they will discover that those who possess little in terms of material wealth have much to return in terms of local know-how, of friendships, and of a readiness to take joint action for the sake of others. When people share in this fashion, they enter into the kind of social relationships for which Richard Tawney coined the word "fellowship" (Terrill, 1974).

Fellowship is not to be confused with the boss having a drink with the workers or with the highly paid welfare director visiting a deprived zone. This is no more like the fellowship of sharing than the Queen doling out Maunday money for it implies the superiority of one party over the other. Fellowship is possible when individuals share the same neighbourhood, leisure institutions and schools; when they are bound together by similar interests; when they both give to and take from each other. Fellowship is about mutual respect and inter-dependence. Fellowship exists when individuals share both their strengths and their weaknesses. Socialism in action is the daily sharing of goods and of selves.

More than Politics
The practice of socialism may involve the taking of lower incomes, the vacating of power and status, and the sharing of possessions and selves. For the socially advantaged such actions may appear

like heavy and costly sacrifices. But there is the compensation of
the closeness formed with others in extending socialism and so
creating a better social environment for all. Tawney called it
fellowship, Lansbury called it love. Towards the end of a lifetime
spent in what he called "dear, ugly East London", Lansbury (1936,
p.15) could still write,

> Yes, I want our people to join me in striving to bring love into all our
> lives, because once we love each other, all other things will be added
> unto us.

I hope that present day socialists will not be ashamed of the
concept of love but rather will experience and express it as they
join with others in bringing about what Helena Born called "the new
time".

The argument put forward in this chapter is not that the
application of socialism to day-to-day life is an alternative to the
political and structural reforms required to re-distribute income,
wealth and power between different social groupings. Hopefully,
a socialist government will gain office and will create the
circumstances which allow socialist values to flourish. But the fact
is that the Labour Party was defeated at the General Election of
1992. If follows that, in the immediate future, one way in which
socialists can express their creed is by the nature of their living.

The effect of individuals upon others should not be underestimated. As indicated at the beginning of this essay, it was Phil
Bashford's personal qualities — his cheerfulness, his capacity to
encourage, his kindness, his unselfishness — which had an impact
on neighbours, friends, colleagues and children. And if socialists
apply the principles of socialism to their daily behaviour then not
only will they become better persons but their characters and
attitudes will be noticed by others. Indeed as in the time of Lansbury,
they will attract them to socialism and so win greater backing for
those social policies which will eventually alter the nature of our
society. Meanwhile, Roy Hattersley's definition of socialism as "the
pursuit of equality and the *protection* of freedom" needs to be
changed to "the *practice* of equality and the *promotion* of freedom
within the framework of daily sharing".

References
Bristol Broadsides, (1984), *Bristol's Other History.*
Dennis N. & Halsey, A.H. (1988) *English Ethical Socialism*, Clarendon Press.
Drabble, M. (1988) *The Case for Equality*, Fabian Society.
Foot, M. (1987) "Ideals and Low Deals", *The Guardian*, 10th April 1987.
Foote, G. (1986) *The Labour Party's Political Thought: A History*, Croom Helm.
Groser, Father St. John (1949) *Politics and Persons*, Student Christian Movement.

Hattersley, R. (1987) *Choose Freedom: the Future for Democratic Socialism*, Michael Joseph.

Holman, B. (1988). *Looking Back*, Plymouth Polytechnic. Available for £2.50 (incl. p+p) from the Phil Bashford Memorial Trust, c/o Keith Popple, Department of Applied Social Science, University of Plymouth, Plymouth PL4 8AA.

Holman, B. (1990) *Good Old George: the Life of George Lansbury*, Lion.

Lansbury, E. (1934) *George Lansbury My Father*, Sampson Low.

Lansbury, G. (1928) *My Life*, Constable.

Lansbury, G. (1936) *My England*, Selwyn & Blount.

Pankhurst, S. (1978) *The Suffragette Movement*, Virago, pp.426-7.

Simmons, J. (1972) *Soap Box Evangelist*, Janay.

Terrill, R. (1974) *R.H. Tawney & His Times: Socialism As Fellowship*, Andre Deutsch.

3

Towards a Progressive Community Work Praxis

Keith Popple

Introduction

Historically community work has developed from two distinct roots: benevolent paternalism and collective community action. The British economic crisis dating from the mid-1970s has gradually led to a lessening of the emphasis on benevolent paternalism and in its place state policy makers have encouraged a regressive form of community work that has emphasised 'care' rather than 'action'. This has taken place by concentrating greater power into the hands of central government while divesting local authorities of many of their meaningful roles (Butcher *et al,* 1989; Blake *et al* 1991) and by introducing a divisive form of financing local services through the poll tax and, at present, the council tax. Government scrutiny to ensure community work projects 'political neutrality' is very much in evidence, with an emphasis on schemes linked with the private sector and an encouragement of self-help and voluntary help (Moore, 1992).

For those whose sympathies lie with collective community action and believe in community work as a liberating progressive force, the task before us during the coming years is to reclaim and revitalise the activity in a manner that reflects and responds to the needs of the socially and economically oppressed. This chapter discusses how it could be possible to achieve this by developing a critical community work theory and practice: a praxis which appreciates the contradictory position of community work within contemporary society. This praxis also recognises that community work is not a fixed form of practice with a static theory, but rather an activity that has to continually redefine and reconstruct itself to critically reflect our changing understanding of peoples' experiences.

The chapter outlines the need for a new debate that builds on our present understandings of community work and which is committed to examine and develop alternatives to current community work policies and practice.

To assist this development I have drawn upon the work of the Italian social theorist Antonio Gramsci, and the Brazilian adult educator Paulo Freire, who in different but complementary ways help us address the theory/practice debate. Gramsci provides us with an understanding of the key concepts of hegemony, ideology, and the role of intellectuals, while Freire has developed the notion of 'conscientization' and the use of particular educational methods to help people to perceive, interpret, criticise and finally transform the world around themselves.

Community Work as an Activity
Before moving into a discussion of a progressive praxis we need to briefly consider the developments that have taken place that have led us to need to prevent the demise of community work's critical edge.

Since the late 1960s community work theory and practice has been influenced by two major approaches: the pluralist, and the radical or socialist.

(a) The pluralist approach:
This approach dominated the debate around modern community work theory and practice from the mid 1940s to the early 1970s and can be seen in the writings of, among others, Batten (1969), Biddle & Biddle (1965), Goetschius (1975), Thomas (1978; 1983), Twelvetrees (1991) and Henderson (1981; 1987). Although primarily concerned with theories of community work practice as opposed to "grand theories" of society, the pluralist approach nevertheless acknowledges the structual nature of deprivation and recognises the political dimension to community work. The focus, however, is on micro change. Since advocates of this approach believe that community work is concerned with social stability and marginal improvements, they emphasise the value of its educational and experimental aspects. In this context education is seen as a means of "enhancing political responsibility" and the equipping of groups and individuals for effective participation.

The pluralist approach has been rather grandly named the "professional school" by Twelvetrees because the advocates tend to emphasise the technical skills and knowledge, such as organisational relationships, action and planned skills, while being eclectic and pragmatic in their strategies. Thomas, for instance, sees clear differences between the trained paid worker and the indigenous community activist and although he states that one type of worker is not "inherently better" than the other, his emphasis on skill training, supervision, and the need for a distinct knowledge base seems to indicate his own position on the matter.

(b) The radical or socialist approach:
Critical of the pluralist model of community work for its negation of a wider political analysis the Community Development Projects, Lees and Mayo (1984), Jacobs (1984), Craig *et al* (1982), Forrest (1984), and Sayer (1986) among several, develop models of theory and practice based on socialist or 'left' radical principles. These practitioners and writers place community work within a struggle for macro change, developing ideas that incorporate the experiences of community action and the labour movement. Jacobs, for instance, argues that socialism needs to re-establish its relationship with working class communities and believes it can do so by examining the lessons learnt from radical community work. Similarly Craig *et al* attempt to develop a radical theoretical base for community work practice. This perspective has further evolved to address issues of race (Ohri *et al*, 1982) and sex equality (Curno *et al* 1982; Dominelli 1990; Flynn *et al*, 1986). The theme of these discussions has been to recognise the disparate experience within the community and the need to tackle structured inequalities at the neighbourhood level.

The Emerging Debate
As we can see the main difference between these two contesting approaches is one of emphasis and commitment. The pluralist approach's emphasis on technical skills is at the expense of a critical appreciation of the changing social, economic and political world or a commitment to being part of any real progressive change. This leads one to believe that the approach is basically a pragmatic one. By concentrating on the marginal gains possible in community work and its role in regard to social stability the pluralist approach fails to make effective theoretical and practice connections between individual's experience and the changing nature of contemporary society. Furthermore, pluralist community work tends to placate rather than liberate the individuals and groups that come within its orbit. It is something that is "done to" rather than determined by a community with the concepts of participatory, non-oppressive and anti-discriminatory ways of working occasionally discussed, even less adopted, and never consistently practised. The pluralist approach promotes the often contested but attractive concept of self-help and self-reliance; a concept that equally appeals to the right, centre and left of the political spectrum. It is a concept

favoured, for instance, by those who believe in an individualist/ laissez-faire approach as well as those who associate themselves with an anarchist anti-statist view.

Trying to walk the centre line, however, the pluralist approach with its focus on marginal change and social stability can, at times, appear to have more in common with the New Right's demand for people to "stand on their own two feet" and engage in voluntary work, than in encouraging collective community activity at the grassroot level.

There are certain themes within the pluralist approach (for instance the importance of appropriate skills) that are important to a revitalised community work praxis but their overall failure to offer a critical analysis and practice leaves them seriously wanting. What progressive community work can offer is a praxis that is committed to working for the deconstruction of the oppressive and unequal relations in our society while reconstructing the opportunities for the plurality of different groups and concerns to effect democratic and sustained change. A plurality that is not dominated by one class or group, but where every group has distinct but equal status.

Community Work and the State

As part of our efforts to develop a progressive community work praxis we must include a note on the activity's relationship with the state which continues to be its major sponsor.

It is no coincidence that British community work emerged as a state activity during the late 1960s when the post-war economic boom began to falter; as people became increasingly disillusioned with the major political parties; with the rise of pressure group politics and protest movements; together with the fear of urban unrest focused primarily around the issue of immigration. Community work was one of a number of interventions that was both co-opted and initiated by the government to diffuse any possible radical protest at a time of economic and social turbulence. With the watch words of consultation and participation very much in evidence the government set about implementing a number of social policies in the fields of education (Plowden 1967), social work (Seebohm 1968), planning (Skeffington 1969) and youth work (Fairbairn-Milson 1969), while launching the Community Development Projects (CDPs) in twelve economically deprived areas, together with the national Urban Aid Programme.

Since the late 1970s radical community workers, who have been influenced by the CDP's reports and the development of a critical emphasis in social policy, have attempted to develop their practice around the key issues inherent in feminism, the black critique and the class analysis, and in turn have moved from a primarily economistic interpretation to one that recognises class recomposition and emerging new concerns and interests.

In the 1980s, Thatcherism exploited the popular discontent with the post-war consensus for welfare, education and housing, and restructured the nature and scope of the welfare state in a far-reaching regressive manner (Hall, 1988). Interestingly and understandably, community work as an occupation enjoyed an expansion during this period. A survey undertaken in 1983 of community workers in the UK indicated 5,000 practitioners were employed at the time, compared with little more than 1,000 in the early 1970s (Francis *et al*, 1984). However, one writer believes this increase was due to many agencies redesignating jobs and adding the term community to their titles; to the state's policy of community care and the resultant

> layer of workers, albeit low-paid, to implement its strategy of shifting the burden of welfare work from public collective to private individual shoulders (Craig, 1989, p.12)

and to the growth in the number of workers required to operate a battery of employment schemes.

The state, then, has been and still is the major funding agency for community work and therefore a strong influence on the scope, focus and direction the work has taken. Increasingly the state has sharpened its understanding and involvement in community work while recognising the contradiction inherent in the relationship. On the one hand the state is required to ensure the profitability of private capital while on the other it has to deal with the impact of capital on those who sell their labour. Community work is one tool amongst many that can be employed to support the dominant ideology that argues that it is possible to solve the problems of the material deprivations and social injustices it has created. It is this fragile contradictory position which provides progressive practitioners with opportunities to work alongside communities and to develop a practice that promotes the empowerment of people by encouraging them to articulate, understand and take action.

Gramsci and the lessons for Community Work
One of the most important thinkers to assist us in further developing our understanding of the state and, in turn, to help us in our work of developing a meaningful praxis for progressive community work is Antonio Gramsci (1881-1937). His writings are particularly useful because they reject the crude historical materialist arguments typical of the Marxist left in the 1960s and 1970s which in turn influenced the CDPs and the radical community work of the period. Instead

Gramsci's work moves us on to consider an analysis of how groups and individuals can shape developments within society. For our consideration here Gramsci's concepts of hegemony, ideology, and intellectuals are the most relevant.

Gramsci discusses the notion that any ruling elite dominates subordinate classes with a combination of force and consent. Force is exercised through the armed forces, the police, the law courts and prisons, while consent is gained through the political, moral and intellectual leadership within the civil society. Maintenance of this domination is achieved by a process of hegemony which has been described as:

> the relation between classes and other social forces. A hegemonic class, or part of a class, is one which gains the consent of other classes and social forces through creating and maintaining a system of alliance by means of political and ideological struggle. (Simon, 1982, p.22).

Gramsci argues that the civil society, which has been defined since as comprising organisations such as political parties, trade unions, churches and cultural, charitable and community groups, is critical in sustaining the hegemony. Civil society is also the sphere where popular-democratic struggles are grouped together, eg. race, gender, age, community, ethnicity, nation and so forth. These struggles have been identified as social movements. Gramsci would further argue that it is within the civil society that the struggle for hegemony takes place between the classes. .

To achieve an effective hegemony there must be a number of shared beliefs or ideas which are generally accepted by all but which serve to justify the interests of the dominant groups. These images, concepts and ideas which "makes sense" of everyday experiences are called ideology. Gramsci argues that ideology is the cement that keeps society together. If you want to change the cement or ideology then you have to work on the institutional levels (Sayer, 1986). However, Gramsci also argues that the subordinate classes (and here Gramscian writers tend to interpret this as the working class) do not necessarily have the conceptual tools to fully comprehend the situation or the means to formulate the radical alternatives to change the ideology or overcome the hegemonic forces. If change is to take place, Gramsci believes that "external agents" in the guise of intellectuals, organisers and leaders are required. Gramsci's definition of intellectuals extends beyond the traditionally held one of thinkers, philosophers, artists, journalists and writers to include organisers such as civil servants and political leaders who are active in civil society, as well as engineers, managers and technicians who function in the production sphere.

Gramsci describes "organic" intellectuals as those who have been created by a particular class and

> which gives it homogeneity and an awareness of its own function not only in the economic but also in the social and political fields. (*Selections from the Prison Notebooks*, 1971, p.5)

These intellectuals are not outside a particular class. On the contrary, they are theorists who are members of the class they represent. Thus a capitalist class creates its own intellectuals in the form of economists, civil servants, industrial managers, writers and media personnel who reflect and support the values of the capitalist system. We have seen that their role is crucial in the civil society where the battle for hegemony is of prime importance. The question we can now pose is: are progressive community workers "organic" intellectuals? Most are employed in one way or another by the state and are therefore acting with particular instructions, or with authority, so that they could be considered to be a subordinate branch of the dominant "organic" intellectuals. On the other hand the very fact they are often at odds with the dominant ideology and are encouraging individuals and groups to articulate their own discourse means they do not acquiesce to the dominant system. Therefore it could be interpreted that they are engaged in assisting in the making and remaking of the conditions necessary for radical social changes.

To assist us understand and clarify the role of community workers in this paradigm we can again refer to Simon (1982) who argues that certain groups of workers are part of an important "middle strata" which have particular professional and corporate interests and traditions. He believes it is the specialised training provided in particular institutions such as colleges which separate the "middle strata" from the vast majority of workers.

> They have been constituted into a variety of "middle strata" capable of playing a distinctive part in politics which can be very significant indeed. They are therefore a vital component of the broad alliance which has to be built up by the working class if it is to achieve a hegemonic role in society. (Simon, 1982, p.98).

The writings of Gramsci and Simon demonstrate that members of this "middle strata" can hold traditional views and act as instruments of political stability. For instance, Gramsci is critical of the conservative role adopted by trade unions and their leaders in working within bourgeois democracy.

Meanwhile he was aware that the present economic and political system does not represent the non-elite and consequently there is always the potential for social disintegration. We can say therefore that the work of community workers in facilitating the response of the non-elite means they have an strategic place within the changing social milieu.

Gramsci's work then offers us a workable framework for our development of a progressive community work theory and practice. As we have seen the dominant class maintains and reproduces its ascendancy through a complex web of ideological processes to attempt to establish one major understanding of reality which is intended to permeate our principles, social relationships, and intellectual and moral positions. However, this understanding is never completely secure because our daily experiences of the world are frequently at odds with the view offered by bourgeois ideology. We can therefore simultaneously hold different and apparently contradictory and inconsistent understandings of the world; one that is determined by the prevailing dominant ideology and the other determined by our everyday experiences in communities which gives us "common sense" knowledge. Community workers are situated in a pivotal position within the civil society for although they are employees of the state and are required to play a part in maintaining the social system, they are not necessarily in agreement with its ideology. Progressive community workers therefore have opportunities to work alongside members of communities as they articulate their contradictory understanding of the world and their situation within it. Progressive community work is also concerned with moving between the terrain of ideas and discussion and into transforming action to change people's material situation.

Now that we have referred to Gramsci to help us establish the nature of the broad process into which community workers are intervening we need to consider how we can help develop a practice that has as its central pivot the concept of "education for change". The most important and influential exponent of this approach is Paulo Freire.

Freire's contribution to progressive community work
Freire (1970; 1972; 1976; 1985) is probably the world's most well known radical adult educator. Born in 1921, Freire's Christianity led him to work with some of the poorest communities in Brazil, but on encountering their social and economic plight he began to adopt a radical position arguing that societies have been constructed for the benefit of the minority through the labours of the majority. Freire's distinct theoretical position stands between two well known radical ones: the new sociology of education, and the tradition of liberation theology. Freire shares with the radicals in the new

sociology of education the analysis that the educational process
transmits both objective knowledge and a hidden curriculum which
supports the dominant culture and class. He does not however share
his colleagues' despair that no change can be made in such an elitist
and selective practice. Working with poverty stricken South
American communities, Freire found that it is possible to develop
approaches by which people can voice their feelings and
experiences. This educational process rejects the traditional
oppressive and hierarchical "banking system" where knowledge is
a commodity to be accumulated in order to gain access to positions
of power and privilege. Instead Freire proposes "education for
liberation" where learners and teachers are engaged in a process
in which abstract and concrete knowledge together with experience
are integrated as praxis. Critical thinking and dialogue (as opposed
to discussion) are fundamental features in this educational process
which seeks to challenge conventional explanations of everyday
life while considering the action necessary for the transformation
of oppressive conditions.

Freire's link with liberation theology is in his philosophy of hope.
He believes that the Kingdom of God is a state that can be created
on earth, but only through a faith in human beings and the necessity
of "permanent struggle".

Freire's extensive writings, which record his unique work and
ideas, centre on the concept of "conscientisation" otherwise known
as politicisation and political action. Before people can engage in
action for change they have first to reflect upon their present
situation. However the nature of ideological domination means that
the oppressed accept, and frequently collude with, the reproduction
of a society's inequalities and the explanations and justifications
offered for the status, power and privilege of their oppressors.
Overcoming this false ideology means overcoming people's
pessimistic and fatalistic thinking, a task not underestimated by
Freire.

Freire argues that educators have to work on the experiences
brought by oppressed people. This entails providing opportunities
for people to validate their experiences, culture, dreams, values and
histories while recognising such expressions carry both the seeds
of radical change and the burden of oppression. Freire's position
coincides with that held by many community workers that it is
necessary to start from a person's own understanding. The skill then,
according to Freire, is to move people by a 'problematising'
approach rather than a 'problem solving' stance as advocated in the
banking system of education.

'Problem solving' involves an expert being distant from a person's reality while engaging in an analysis that efficiently resolves difficulties before dictating a strategy or policy. Freire believes this reduces human experience and difficulties to that which can be 'treated'. 'Problematising' however means immersing oneself in the struggles of oppressed people and in engaging in the task

> of codifying total reality into symbols which can generate critical consciousness (Freire, 1976, p.ix)

which then empowers people to begin to alter their social relations. This is undertaken by a process of critical reflection, then action, followed by further critical reflection and further action. This creates the conditions for the development of genuine theory and collective action because both are rooted in a historical and cultural reality. Freire, however, believes that theory and practice are not collapsible one with another, arguing for a distance between the two. To quote Henry A. Giroux:

> Theory does not dictate practice; rather, it serves to hold practice at arm's length in order to mediate and critically comprehend the type of praxis needed within a specific setting at a particular time in history. (Freire, 1985, p.xxiii)

Community work has much to learn from the work of Freire for he rejects the stance often taken by practitioners when they mediate between the oppressed and the oppressors. As one writer observes, community workers may have a philosophy and practice that assists people to articulate their concerns and to be more involved in their communities, but these activities

> continue to be framed or defined by those who already hold power rather than constituting real challenges to and transformations of that frame. (Allman, 1987, p.220)

As we have seen, progressive community work is not a mediating process between the oppressed and oppressors but is a liberating force that recognises the inherent contradictions in capitalism while providing a practice that centres on developing a critical dialogue and increasing a political consciousness. Freire's work, with its emphasis on 'tuning in' to the learner's world, provides us with examples of how essential critical reflection and action, ie. praxis, is to community work.

Gramsci and Freire: a hopeful analysis and practice
The intention of this chapter has been to outline the need to reclaim and revitalise progressive community work from the advocates of

the New Right. This means moving from the debates of pluralist versus radical that typified the 1970s and 1980s to establishing a new praxis that is rooted in people's everyday experiences while recognising the changing nature of contemporary society. As we have noted, the two most helpful writers and practitioners in this cause are Gramsci and Freire who in different yet similar ways offer us a workable and hopeful analysis and practice.

Both have attracted the criticisms that their work is located in a different age (as in the case of Gramsci) or their work is not transferable to the developed world (as in the case of Freire). Critics, however, miss the universality of both writers, while trying to make their work fit exactly in a different time or context. The very essence of both Gramsci's and Freire's work is that it is not intended to be adopted in a rigid uncritical way. What is central to both writers is their understanding of the struggle between elite and non-elite groups, wherever they are found.

Conclusion
There is every possibility that the inherent British economic crisis will continue and recur during this decade. Only a major social restructuring and a new kind of political settlement, together with a massive economic investment in education, training, industry and the welfare state will prevent us becoming a minor European outpost with worsening public services, savage and increasingly unequal concentrations of private wealth, and a profoundly undemocratic electoral system. In this event, traditional community work agencies will play a strategic role as a buffer between a regressive centralised state that has eroded the autonomy and scope of local authorities, and poor and potentially disruptive communities. Community work will then become synonymous with community care and the delivery of inadequate services to the most vulnerable in our society.

For many of us, however, community work is a progressive force that is engaged in liberating the minds, and encouraging and supporting the actions of the disadvantaged. This chapter has highlighted the possibilities for developing a rigorous, progressive community work praxis that utilises the work of Gramsci and Freire and supports a more just, democratic and humane vision of society. If progressive community work is to be a credible force it will require a concerted, creative effort against regressive attempts to use the activity to further subordinate the very people who finance our wages. However, the prospective reward for those involved in this process, is to be a practitioner in a dynamic and thriving community work practice that reflects and addresses the need to reshape our society.

References

Allman, P., (1987) 'Paulo Freire's education: a struggle for meaning' in Allen, G., Bastiani, J., Martin, I., Richards, K., *Community Education. An agenda for educational reform*. Buckingham: Open University Press.

Batten, T.R. (1967) with the collaboration of Madge Batten, *The Non-Directive Approach in Group and Community Work*. Oxford: Oxford University Press.

Biddle, L. & Biddle, W. (1965) *The Community Development Process: The Re-discovery of Local Initiative*. New York: Holt, Rinehart and Winston.

Blake, B., Bolan, P. and Burns, D., edited by Gaster, L. (1991) *Local Budgeting in Practice: Learning from two case studies*. Decentralisation Research and Information Centre Report 3. Bristol: School for Advanced Urban Studies, Bristol.

Butcher, H., Law, I.G., Leach, R., Mullard, M., (1990) *Local Government and Thatcherism*. London: Routledge.

Craig, G. (1989) 'Community Work and the State', *Community Development Journal*. 24(1) 3-18.

Craig, G., Derricourt, M., and Loney, M. (eds) (1982) *Community Work and the State: towards a radical practice*. London: Routledge and Kegan Paul in association with the Association of Community Workers.

Curno, A., Lamming, A., Leach, L., Stiles, J., Ward, V., and Ziff, T. (1982) *Women in Collective Action*, Newcastle upon Tyne: Association of Community Workers.

Dominelli, L. (1990) *Women and Community Action*. Birmingham: Venture Press.

Fairbairn & Milson (1969) *Youth and Community Work in the 70s*. London: HMSO.

Flynn, P., Johnson, C., Liberman, S., and Armstrong, H. (1986) *You're Learning All the Time: Women, Education and Community Work*. Nottingham: Spokesman.

Forrest, D., (1984) 'Marxism and the community worker' *Association of Community Workers Talking Point, 50*. Available from ACW, Stephenson Building, Elswick Road, Newcastle-upon-Tyne, NE4 6SQ.

Francis, D., Henderson, P., Thomas, D.N. (1984) *A Survey of Community Workers in the United Kingdom*. London: National Institute of Social Work.

Freire, P. (1970) *Cultural Action for Freedom*. Harmsworth: Penguin.

Freire, P. (1972) *Pedagogy of the Oppressed*. Harmsworth: Penguin.

Freire, P. (1976) *Education: The Practices of Freedom*. London: Writers and Readers Publishing Cooperative.

Freire, P. (1985) *The Politics of Education. Culture, Power and Liberation*. London: Macmillan.

Geotschius, G. (1975) 'Some difficulties in introducing a community work option into social work training', in Jones, D. and Mayo, M. (eds) *Community Work Two*. London: Routledge.

Hall, S. (1988) *The Hard Road to Renewal: Thatcherism and the Crisis of the Left*. London. Verso.

Henderson, P., and Thomas, D.N. (1981) *Readings in Community Work*. London: Allen & Unwin.

Henderson, P., and Thomas, D.N. (1987) *Skills in Neighbourhood Work* (2nd edition). London: Allen & Unwin.

Jacobs, S., (1984) 'Community Action and the building of Socialism from below: a defence of the non-directive approach', *Community Development Journal*. Vol.19 No.4. Oxford University Press.

Lees, R., and Mayo, M., (1984) *Community Action for Change*. London: Routledge

& Kegan-Paul.

Moore, B., (1992) 'Taking on the Inner Cities' in Michie, J. (ed.) *The Economic Legacy 1979-1992.* London: Academic Press.

Ohri, A., Manning, B., and Curno, P. (eds) (1982) *Community Work and Racism.* London: Routledge and Kegan Paul in association with the Association of Community Workers.

Plowden (1967) *Children and their Primary Schools.* London: HMSO.

Sayer, J., (1986) 'Ideology: The Bridge Between Theory and Practice' in *Community Development Journal,* Vol.21 No.4, Oxford University Press.

Seebohm Report (1968) Report of the Committee on Local Authority and Allied Personal Social Services. Cmnd 3703 London: HMSO.

Selections from the Prison Notebooks, (1971) edited and translated by Hoare, Q. and Nowell Smith, G. London: Lawrence and Wishart.

Simon, R. (1982) *Gramsci's Political Thought.* London: Lawrence and Wishart.

Skeffington (1969) *People and Planning.* London: HMSO.

Thomas, D.N. (1983) *The Making of Community Work.* London: George Allen and Unwin.

Thomas, D.N. (1978) 'Community Work, social change and social planning' in Curno, P. (ed.) *Political Issues and Community Work.* London: Routledge.

Twelvetrees, A. (1991) *Community Work* (2nd Edition). London: Macmillan.

4

From Black British to Black European: a Crisis of Identity?

Ranjit Sondhi

This chapter is concerned with the birth, growth, and, on occasions, the paralysis of community projects that use ethnicity as a basis for radical grouping. It attempts to place their evolution within a post-war historical context following the failure of the established left to produce any coherent agenda for social change. It raises the issue of the re-incarnation of ethnicity since the late seventies as a prologue to the destructive ethnic nationalism in Europe in the nineties. It traces the progressive detachment of the 'community' from the state, and marks the dilemma faced by black self-help initiatives in monetarist Britain since 1979. Finally, it looks forward into the mid and late nineties and examines the position of British "ethnics" within the boundaries of a larger disintegrating Europe, and questions whether radical free market theory holds any salvation for black people who live a life marred by discrimination and degradation both here and abroad.

Post-War Britain and the Growth of Black Community Projects
Even before the Second World War, it had become increasingly clear that the left in Britain had abandoned any serious attempt to present a genuine socialist challenge to modern capitalism. Together with the general failure of the Labour Party to voice the grievances and demands of working people, and its assimilation into the orthodox structures of British society, radical thought and action were channelled into *single* issue campaigns such as those around world hunger, colonial freedom, nuclear disarmament, child poverty, homelessness, and racial equality/justice (Williams, 1968). In the face of the structure of a new capitalism, and the machinery of managed politics that drove it, such a splintering of concern for the casualties of the economic system was inevitable.

In themselves these diverse campaigns provided a refreshing change from the tired and predictable styles of all brands of left-wing socialism. Those in Britain in the late sixties found resonance in and picked up momentum from the cataclysmic events happening elsewhere in the world — the student revolutions in Europe, the growing protests against the Vietnam war, the rise of the black struggle and of black power in the United States. These campaigns were not the product of romantic imaginations or charismatic leadership. They were based on an analysis of social realities in the day-to-day life of the vast majority of people in Britain: at work, in education, housing, health, and social welfare. These analyses revealed — often startlingly to sober British minds — gross and intolerable areas of poverty and inequality in a system where the majority of people found it difficult to exercise any direct control over their lives. The practical programme that followed this analysis demanded a shift from working for reform through the orthodox channels of parliamentary democracy to a kind of 'neighbourhood' politics in which people could participate in decisions on issues that directly influenced them.

As a consequence, since the late 1960s, particularly in the socio-cultural sphere, community action projects were initiated in areas of multiple deprivation which were characterised by rising levels of unemployment, decaying housing, over-crowded schools, over-burdened social services, and poor recreation facilities — a deprivation that was brought into sharper and more uncomfortable focus by the arrival and settlement of black workers and their families drawn in from the vast ex-colonial reserves of Asia and the Caribbean. Typically, this black presence was presented as the central cause of inner city decay, and as the major threat to the already stretched fabric of British working class life. However, as the crisis of Britain was translated into the crisis of race, and the dream of assimilation was finally buried, black people began to take up positions that were both defiant and defensive. Under these circumstances even the most open and multi-cultural community projects had only a limited attraction for black people. They chose instead to operate within their own microcosm characterised by distinct cultural and linguistic boundaries beyond which they suffered from an unease that had its roots in centuries of colonial exploitation and oppression. Multi-racial neighbourhood initiatives of the early 1970s failed to make black people feel at ease, because the most well-intentioned and ideologically sound attempts at bringing people together in collective action were invariably set against the background of sustained hostility towards black people, issuing from all sections of a class society and many of its major institutions.

It was in this social milieu — even as the hysteria about race rose frequently to a screaming pitch with moral panics over black crime and immigrants flooding into the country — that there began to develop in the black sector, an active political ideology which used ethnicity as a basis for radical grouping. This was accompanied by a conscious, sometimes unconscious, need to withdraw from the mainstream of white working class life. Against the criticism that this amounted to a system of 'self-imposed apartheid' that would dissipate a collective challenge to the existing system still further, there was a legitimate case to be put forward for building up powerful self-images through a tactical withdrawal, prior to any effective involvement in the life of the wider community.

The ideological position was that in an open democratic society relations between majority and minority communities should involve the preservation of two fundamental principles. The first should be *equal participation* for individuals, every citizen, irrespective of his/her membership of a minority group, ought to be able to participate equally in the larger society. The second would be *self determination* for groups, members of every minority ought to be able to participate fully in the distinctive cultural enterprises that contribute to their identity. The tension between these two principles could roughly be captured in the apparent paradox — equal in public but different in private. However, while the realisation of equal participation required radical structural change, which would not be brought about by minority struggle alone, self determination appeared a more realisable ideal as it depended largely upon developing the relationship between the individual and her/his cultural grouping in isolation from the workings of wider society. Self-determination was to be the strategic first step before the question of equal participation could be effectively addressed. However, black community projects often reflected the tension between the two principles, in their statement of aims and objectives. For example, in the Asian Resource Centre, Handsworth, Birmingham, these were:

(a) to identify and analyse the cultural and structural restraints placed upon particular minority groups in the neighbourhood; and,

(b) to initiate, participate in and assist projects designed to protect their rights, encourage freedom of cultural expression and promote a strong sense of ethnic pride. (Asian Resource Centre, 1979)

It was this strategic revival of ethnicity that was exhilarating, dynamic and promising. Ethnicity was not just a heightened sense of cultural awareness. It was a much more complex process which resulted, as Orlando Patterson described:

> From the interplay of two kinds of social concourses; an inner, inter-objective concourse between the individual and we-group; and an outer structural concourse involving the individual/we-group on the one hand, and on the other, the wider world or out-group. The *inner* concourse begins with consciousness of a shared crisis of alienation resolved through a commitment to the group sharing the crisis, one symbolically validated as a large endogamous kindred with a common memory. The *outer* concourse takes account of the source of the crisis, its content and timing, the resources of the potential group, the arithmetic of its social relations with wider society and the policy of its leadership. Specific configurations of these two sets of factors determine the kind of ethnic movement and resulting ethnic group. (Fried 1983: 25)

It was this intricate interplay between biography, culture and structure that gave this original concept of ethnicity — developed in the bosom of black struggle — its essential vibrancy and appeal. By the early 1980's, however, the gap between the idea of ethnicity as a basis for radical reform and the practical programmes that followed was rapidly widening. Ethnicity — like race had been earlier — was beginning to be associated with a set of immutable characteristics — a thing in itself and *not* a process — that would be passed on in a deterministic way from one generation to the next. Ethnicity was being perceived as the one difference that made all the difference. The consciousness of *race* and *ethnicity* which begins as a powerful means of organising and resisting — ended in all too many cases as a means of mystifying and deflecting.

Single issue campaigns contain within them the power to question the whole politics of the system in the light of the single issue. But they also contain the seeds of their own destruction. It was inevitable that all such 'ethnic' groups and initiatives — like all other groups that come together on the basis of language, religion or national sentiment — would eventually face crises of direction and of internal policy. There would inevitably be people to oppose within their own ethnic group and people to align with from outside. Black people might need to align with white people against other blacks. Paradoxically, the test of any single issue campaign in the existing political system is the point at which it appears to fail. When the question arrives whether complete success is possible without a challenge to the whole structure, black groups face a crucial dilemma. Either they remain as a focus for dissent, with the attendant and ever-present danger of being used as a 'safety valve', or they push the issue right through to a point where they contradict their own definition and remain not a single movement but transform into a general campaign.

This is not to diminish the fact that in Britain black communities continue to live out more sharply than any other identifiable group, the whole range of deep and sustained social deprivation in the decaying inner city, in overcrowded schools, in bad housing, in low wages of unskilled work, in a growing and virulent youth unemployment. Yet this general problem, which is imposed in differing intensity on other groups of dispossessed people, is being *displaced* by the revival of ethnicity. The fact that people are black, or ethnic, is seized upon to confuse and deflect. Class consciousness is displaced by ethnic consciousness and the problems of society are being presented as a special detachable problem between black and white.

It is a sober reminder of the power of forces external to the community groups to define, modify, constrain or promote as required the internal dynamic of unity or disunity within any particular ethnic grouping.

The 1980s

During the 1980s we witnessed an exponential increase in the number of projects dealing with specific issues within the black community, whether these were concerned with mother tongue teaching, cultural provisions, religious instruction, special schools or ethnic music and dance. It was, of course, entirely appropriate to cater for such singular needs but they cannot not be conceived as separate or even separable components of the sum total of the condition of life of black working people. By dealing with them in this isolated way it becomes possible to overlook the structural situation and deal with 'local' issues without having to tackle the more fundamental problems that face black people in the wider society. The fact that increasing amounts of public funds were made available to meet these discrete, apparently unrelated needs, raised the question of the role of the state in the affairs of the community.

Workers in such black and ethnic projects may have been empirically only too aware of the effects of the declining economic spiral, the interface between local and national politics, and the place of community action within all this, but may not always have had a well-defined theory of state and community. The pluralist method of state intervention through the funding of a range of diverse ethnic organisations and groups could be identified as a political and ideological use of ethnicity within a particular societal model i.e. one in which the state is *not* neutral, and has an interest in particular forms of 'community relations'.

These community relations have, until recently, to do with pushing the focus of concern away from an institutional to an individual pathology, to steering issues away from the public into the private domain by trading self determination for equal participation and shifting the burden of social welfare from the state to the individual. Multi-culturalism/multi-ethnicism has now become one of the major ideological weapons in the state armoury, to produce on the ground the semblance of equality between the races through an active ethnic renaissance, even as the rights of all citizens — black and white — are gradually eroded. There is now a proliferation of projects specifically designed — and attracting generous state funding — for Afro-Caribbeans and Asians separately, for Hindus, Muslims, Sikhs and Seventh Day Adventists, for exclusive and exclusivist cultural, social and linguistic groups. Racism awareness programmes, so popular in institutions, reinforce the 'immutable' differences between black and white people. Ethnic groups are differentiated even more finely along religious and national lines and 'ethnic leakage' incurs disapproval and ostracism on all sides. The term 'Blacks' has now become 'Blacks and Asians' and even sociologists have given this shift a respectable seal of approval.

Another significant 'shift' is worth noting in state policy in respect of community and citizenship. The then Home Secretary, Douglas Hurd M.P., wrote in the *Church Times* on 9 September 1988:

> Services which are financed by the State are not always best delivered through the State. Education and housing — as well as crime prevention — private enterprise and charitable sector can often meet local needs and local difficulties in a way that the bureaucratic and inflexible agencies of either central or local government find impossible. The active citizen is being invited to the centre of the stage.

More recently this thinking has crystallised into Mr Major's Citizens' Charter. This must surely sound like a worthy clarion call to all citizens to get involved in the life of their community. But even as the virtues of voluntarism are being sung, the political agenda remains transparently clear. The 'caring role' which has been the clear remit of statutory authorities since the Second World War, has in the 1990s been inexorably shifting into the voluntary sector, so that the welfare apparatus of the state can be progressively dismantled. Voluntary agencies, which once railed against the failure of socialist governments and systems to deliver appropriate services, suddenly find themselves uncomfortably juxtaposed with their ideological opponents. The radical campaigns — including some black organisations — are unexpectedly, involuntarily in bed with the radical Right. Even the language achieved congruence so that when Thatcher's 'self-help' or Major's 'active citizenship' are mentioned one has to enquire who is using these terms, as they are capable of taking on diametrically opposite meanings in different ideological contexts. It is particularly disappointing that an opportunity was missed in the Citizen's Charter to back up the general emphasis on avoiding discrimination with an explicit lead on race matters. There is considerable cynicism, even among moderate circles, in the Government's ability to convert the overall aims of the Charter into action programmes to eliminate racial discrimination.

It was stated earlier that with regard to minority groups there was a tension between the pair of principles — that of self determination and equal participation — that pull in opposite directions. At the best of times it is difficult to maintain a balance between the need to maintain a distinctive identity and the right to be considered an equal citizen. Under a relentless programme of re-ethnification, brought about by a combination of internal and external mechanisms, this balance was virtually impossible to strike. But even as the black communities reeled under the worst effects of ethnification the ground was shifting again beneath their feet. Class consciousness had earlier been replaced by ethnic consciousness — now ethnic consciousness itself was to be substituted with an 'individual' consciousness based on the central and seductive notion of self interest. The communitarian view of minority rights in which the group is an expression of a common identity was to be replaced by the aggregative view in which the minority is no more than a *collection* of people, each of whom holds individual rights and is bound by specific obligations. As Mrs Thatcher had said, "There is no such thing as society".

The 1990s and the Black Community
The dilemma for the black community worker is in the recognition that a minority group exists both in the organic and aggregative sense. For black people living in potentially hostile majority communities, the concepts of *community* and *identity* hold a special meaning and potency.

Black people fragmented into ever decreasing ethnic compartments, are rendered vulnerable in the free market world of Conservatism and Europe. In the market place, collectivism bows out to individualism. The multi-culturalism that rose like a saviour from the burnt out hearts of the inner city is now to be laid to rest, a dismantled relic of the past. Despite a lukewarm opposition at the top, Britain will move towards Europe in the 1990s as the western world enters a new economic phase — marked by the reconstruction of capital and deconstruction of labour. Speaking at a national conference on '1992 and the Black Community' in Birmingham, Euro M.P. Christine Crawley made it quite clear that the Single European Act should be seen for what it is:

> the codification of a right wing philosophy of radical free marketing to deregulate Europe's economy in the interest of big business. (Crawley, 1989)

There is to be no special consideration in this expanded market place for the 'British' black with his/her historically specific background. Ethnocentricity will find an easy hiding place in Eurocentricity, and in the world of the EC, racism once again will return to its earlier primitive form where, in the words of Sivanandan:

> it cannot tell one black from another, a citizen from an immigrant, an immigrant from a refugee — and classes all Third World peoples as immigrants and refugees and all immigrants and refugees as terrorists and drug dealers. (Sivanandan, 1988)

This is not to suggest that in the single market of Europe, post-1992, there will be an unprecedented tide of racism spilling over from across the continent to make the position of black people here intolerable. Britain has its own unique blend of homegrown racism carefully cultivated through several hundred years of imperial history to match any of the imported variety. But a spread there will be, no doubt — in both directions — to transform a perfectly respectable British racism to a perfectly respectable European one. A community that operates on the principles of a free market is required to construct a labour force that is suited to its particular economic system, and maintains the balance of black and white workers through the operation of immigration and nationality laws, rules and regulations. Racism is the control mechanism that both legitimises and confines the black, the immigrant, the Third World labour force within social and political boundaries both in the United Kingdom and Europe. The pressure will be on to co-ordinate rules on entry, residency, access to employment and entitlement to civic rights. The major effect of such 'harmonisation' of immigration control both *before* and *after* entry will inevitably be a levelling down process, with controls becoming stricter *not* more liberal. Britain's insistence that her immigration control is not a matter on which the European Community can legislate is based on an anxiety that the sophisticated mechanisms in place to control the entry of black migrants into the UK will be undermined. But while Britain may have a thing or two to teach European countries about how to control entry at *source* through the use of legislation (eg. the use of patriality) and bureaucratic delay, countries like Germany and France would provide the lead on altogether cruder *internal* controls. Their methods already include regular checks on immigration status by employers, random checks by police in the streets, and checks on people applying for benefits and public services. Identity cards will, in future, no longer be reserved for football fans.

The problem for Britain, as for Europe, is that both in a historical and contemporary sense black workers are a 'necessary evil'. Such pronouncements are not proclaimed from Party Headquarters, Whitehall or Westminster, they are uttered in hushed tones in the private corridors of power. It is not part of public policy to admit either that they are necessary (in the economic sense) *or* that they are evil (in the social sense) for fear of hurting working and middle class sensibilities respectively. Britain has now spent over four decades trying to reconcile their economic desirability with their social undesirability, and has moved progressively towards immigration control mechanisms that are designed to systematically reduce *settlement* status while at the same time leaving the door slightly ajar through which potential workers might be allowed to enter and then be ejected when they are no longer economically active. It has been a question of designing an entry policy that allows this country to have the maximum benefit of their labour power but none of their social demands. Other countries in Europe, like Germany, who never suffered from a romantic yearning for a lost Empire, did not from the outset entertain settlement status for workers from their ex-colonies and operated instead a guest worker system that relied on a periodic rotation of a seasonal foreign migrant labour force.

Now, in the throes of a silicon chip revolution, Britain, like all other affluent states in the European market, will argue that it is rational to seal off its community to prevent any erosion of the economic, cultural and political conditions that have been achieved on the basis that they owe it to the vast majority of their (largely white) voters to provide them with such protection. But there is no denying what these policies on entry restrictions really are — a collective device to prevent the redistribution of existing world resources to the benefit of the disadvantaged.

The same technological revolution that results in the Western countries sealing off their boundaries also requires an internal restructuring of the economic framework within which the position of the black worker and European racism might be discussed.

Perhaps the most fundamental point to be made is that this revolution does not obliterate the working class, it merely transforms it. Even as capital is restructured and redistributed across Europe and indeed further afield, so the labour force is similarly reconstructed. What the new economy needs and creates are small cores of highly skilled workers who are able and versatile enough to handle a range of tasks, while the rest of the labour force is pushed to the periphery, or discarded. This process affects black workers disproportionately more than whites. The long grim line of black workers disappearing into foundries and heavy metal industries before the break of dawn to reappear only after overtime in the night is a thing of the past. It is out of these 'rejects' that a new servant class is created — the free marketeers, one-man bands, set up in business to serve the needs of the professional and monied classes as their car valets, their gardeners, pizza-delivery boys, satellite antennae installers and mobile hairdressers. It is the rise of the new entrepreneur, fighting in a fiercely competitive world for custom, to win back a degree of self respect recurring from the prospects of a lifetime of unemployment.

But there is also the dirty work to be done — and of course there are still the blacks around. Sivanandan (1988) mentions Gunter Wallraff, a German journalist living in the guise of an illegal Turkish worker, who exposes the kind of work that such people are lured to do — from cleaning blocked lavatories on building sites "ankle-deep in piss and covered in racist graffiti", to clearing up nuclear power plants "so they can return home before the radiation takes effect". It is racism that allows this to continue, and keeps such exploitation from the public gaze, to absolve a government that wants their labour but none of the responsibilities.

Conclusion
In conclusion, the notion of a free market that is so fundamental to a single Europe needs to be more closely examined. It is assumed in some quarters, black and white, that greater competition not only makes for better quality but also brings more 'players' onto the field. Certainly an influential report of the Commission on Citizenship regards it as axiomatic:

> the virtues of the self-reliant individual in competition with fellow individuals. (Commission on Citizenship, 1989)

If the market is extended across the length and breadth of Europe, who knows what benefits it will bring for private enterprise, regardless of race or nationality! To be sure, capitalism is colour-blind. In addition, liberal free market theory states that free market competition is not only supposed to be the most efficient and effective way of satisfying consumer demands but market competition is the *only* way in which real equality of opportunities can emerge. It is a very seductive proposition especially for those black people for whom self-enterprise is the only perceived option. There are two very questionable assumptions in this theory. The first is that it holds 'justice' and 'fairness' to be relatively sturdy while 'bigotry' and 'prejudice' are comparatively weak, the former prevailing over the latter. In fact, the reverse might be a more likely outcome — it has been said that lies are often more reassuring than truth. The second assumption is that the market can *guarantee* a wholesome society. But markets are just as prone to deliver different brands of racism, sexism, bigotry and xenophobia as supermarkets are prone to deliver 'junk food'. As Professor Newton (1988) remarks, to combine free market competition with the triumph of justice, fairness, impartiality and equality is to aggrandise the theory and to insinuate into the argument something it was not designed to handle in the first place.

Liberal free market theory also assumes that the ordinary citizen is serious and intelligent and sufficiently concerned about justice and fair play. There is now enough known about the human mind to understand how it selects, distorts and subverts what it does not wish to know. The truth is that the European population is as unintelligent and politically illiterate about the subject of race as the British population has been. From 1992 there will indeed be a movement of black and white people across the frontiers, each one looking for new opportunities but this alone will not dispel the racist ideologies that thrive and seriously impair the quality of life for black communities everywhere. Black Britons are as likely to fail in the countries of Europe as other black Europeans are likely to fail in Britain.

A free market requires the removal of all structures so that the individual is free to prosper. But in an unequal society the removal of structure is as much to the benefit of the rich and strong as it is to the detriment of the poor and weak. Those intoxicated on free market theories and who are so earnestly calling for the deregulation of all structures would do well to recall that is was precisely the existence of such structures that allowed them to succeed above their fellow citizens. For an overwhelming majority of black people free market theories do not liberate them from, but further confines them to their specific position within the industrial and social spheres.

There remains a question of whether the Social Charter — introduced in 1988 as a political initiative to introduce a 'social dimension' into a debate hitherto conducted solely in terms of commercial markets and therefore only of concern to business people — is a liberating development. The Charter contained objectives on the right to freedom of movement; employment and remuneration; the improvement of living and working conditions; the right to social protection; the right to freedom of association and collective bargaining; the right to information, consultation and participation for workers; health and safety; the protection of children and adolescents; the treatment of elderly people and people with disabilities. John Wrench suggests

> that as black people are over represented in the worst jobs, the worst pay and conditions, then they are likely to benefit from anything which assists in the campaign to set minimum standards of pay and employment conditions. (Wrench, 1990)

However the likelihood of any real and widespread improvement in the living and working conditions of black people in Europe has to be considered against two factors:
(1) the harsh reality of increasingly restrictive immigration control in Germany, France, Denmark, Belgium, The Netherlands and, of course, Britain;
and
(2) the alarming rise of racism and fascism across the face of Europe. In *'Fortress Europe: the meaning of 1992'*, Paul Gordon catalogues the instances of racial violence that have reached almost epidemic proportions against Turks, Moroccans, Ghanains, and Algerians in Europe while neo-nazi parties are polling increasing numbers of votes. There is growing concern that no collective political will exists to prevent racism becoming an increasingly destructive force in European politics. Black people view with alarm how the stance of more liberal politicians is adjusted to take account of pressures from public 'heroes' like Le Pen. The emergence of neo-fascists in parts of continental Europe, the racist posturing of some presidential candidates in the United States, and the horrific events in Yugoslavia are all evidence of the powerful forces that generate racial conflict. Yet the issue of black people has been consistently ignored or shrugged off in official discussions. It is significant to note that the groups within the Commission working on immigration control either work in secret — like the Trevi Group — or have a decision-making process that is difficult to follow for outsiders — like the Schengen Group.

Of course, the Social Charter does not enjoy unanimous support. Mrs. Thatcher, for one, condemned it as a 'Socialist Charter'. Her opposition, since maintained by John Major, was based on what it contains. Black people's opposition is based on what it does not contain — that is, no clear commitment to an anti-racist society free from intimidation and exploitation of black workers. Rejection of the Social Charter on these grounds is not tantamount to adopting a Thatcherite/Major position on restoring British sovereignty, but acknowledges that the Social Charter will not liberate black workers by itself — just as the Race Relations Act and Equal Opportunities Act has not got rid of discrimination — unless there is a *political* will to do so. More liberal opinion regards it as a matter of regret that the British Government did not sign the Social Chapter at Maastricht as this might weaken Britain's capacity to influence Europe-wide policies in areas which significantly affect the lives of racial minorities. It is to be noted that neither the Treaty of Rome nor the European Convention on Human Rights of the Council of Europe produce explicit protection against racial discrimination — in the face of which Britain's domestic legislation (Race Relations Act 1976), though much in need of reform, looks well in advance of its European partners.

One of the clearest and most unequivocal positions on the condition of life of black people, and the strategies required to ameliorate it, is declared in the European Manifesto 1989 prepared by the Refugee Forum and the Migrants Action Network. It saw 1992 as an opportunity to forge closer alliances with black communities throughout Europe, to form a co-ordinated resistance movement around ten points of direct concern to all immigrants, migrant and refugee communities. These are:

● the right to stay
● the right to family reunion
● free movement in the EEC
● full social and political rights
● full legal rights
● fight against racism, fascism and police brutality
● fight against economic racism
● fight against repatriation and deportation
● right to organise independently
● amnesty for all unauthorised workers.

As a grassroots movement, they declare the need to join together with 'faith communities, base communities and black groups; with trade unions and with political and labour movement organisations' to maximise publicity and support. They certainly feel strongly that the future is not to shrink back into a narrow nationalism but to fight for democracy and liberty in every European country including their own.

Until such movements begin to take effect, for black people *outside* it will be 'Fortress Europe', with a limited number of drawbridges that will be lowered as often to recruit temporary cheap labour from the Third World as to expel a spent labour force. The pre-election Asylum Bill was therefore re-presented by the Government with only minor amendments and became the 1993 Asylum Act. For black people *inside,* they have become subjects of the 'Thirteenth State'.

References

Asian Resource Centre (1979) Progress Report.

Commission on Citizenship (1989) Draft Report.

Crawley, C. (1989) Birmingham Conference.

Gordon, P. (1989) *Fortress Europe: the meaning of 1992.* Runnymeade Trust

Newton, K. (1988) Essex Papers in Politics & Government, No.53, November.

Patterson, O. (1983) in Fried, C. *Community and Identity. Dahlem Conference* Springer-Verlag, pg.25.

Sivanandan, A. (1988) 'The New Racism' in *New Statesman & Society*, November.

Williams, R. (1968) *Mayday Manifesto*, Penguin.

Wrench, J. (1990) 'Employment and the Labour Market' — in *New Community.* Vol.16, No.2, January.

5

Women, Community Work and the State in the 1990s

Lena Dominelli

Women are crucial players in the community work arena, though their contribution as activists and as the people working behind the scenes to enable the 'show to go on' has been scarcely acknowledged in the community work literature (Hanmer and Statham, 1989). Francis and Henderson (1992), Butcher (1992) and the Journal of Community Development provide examples of recent writings on community work which barely mention the relevance of gender politics to community workers and their practice. Sadly, the continued invisibility of women's contribution to community work *per se* is also reflected in the latest feminist writings on social work practice (see Langan and Day, 1992, for example). Yet, power relations between men and women have been critical in defining the roles women have been able to assume in community work, the areas they work in and status accorded such work, and whether they can juggle family responsibilities to participate as activists (Curno *et al.*, 1982; Dominelli and McLeod, 1989; Dixon *et al.*, 1982). However, women's relationship to community work is not only affected by their position *vis-a-vis men*, it is also mediated by their relationship with the state.

The relationship between women, community work and the state has been shrouded in ambiguity and contradictions for some time (Wilson, 1977; Dominelli, 1990). Women have sought state sponsored community work posts to secure waged employment that would provide a modicum of economic independence and resources. But, they have discovered the job opportunities on offer have continued to reinforce their position in the lower paid echelons of society, doing work commonly regarded as 'women's work' or 'soft' community work (Dominelli, 1990). Additionally, the state has drawn on community work techniques to launch major policy initiatives which have reaffirmed women's place as unpaid carers in the community, for example, community care (Finch, 1984) and community based job creation schemes like the Community

Programme which have provided low paid community work. Consequently, women community workers employed within a statutory agency such as a social services department have been appointed at the front line in low waged work alongside women field social workers whilst men occupy managerial posts (Hanmer and Statham, 1989). Thus, women's subordinate status was being reinforced and legitimated through the very avenue that promised an escape route.

The state has also reinforced white heterosexual familialist norms and the primacy of women's domestic labour, particularly as carers of children and elders, by cutting back on public services for the young and old alike and promoting policies which impose substantial caring responsibilities on women within families as part of its community organisation plans aimed at linking community resources with statutory ones through community care policies, street warden schemes, patch systems, and neighbourhood based work (Ungerson, 1991).

Community work skills and processes are being extensively used to implement this policy through unpaid voluntary and poorly paid waged labour. This has become a method through which the state exploits women's energies for the common good and legitimates the division of the world into the private sphere located in the community, allegedly outside its scrutiny and the public sphere which forms its prime site for intervention. But, reality does not operate according to the familialist ideology being fostered by the New Right, and as feminists have revealed, the private and the public spheres are intimately connected and interdependent (Gamarnikov *et al*, 1983). Feminists have used this knowledge to redefine private life and by bringing private matters into the public domain through woman centred community action drawing on feminist campaigns and networks, have turned private matters into social issues, for example, domestic violence, child sexual abuse (Dominelli and McLeod, 1989).

Moreover, the state as a major employer of women has also been the main source of unemployment for women. The axing of full-time posts necessitated by public expenditure cuts has led to their jobs being either abolished or replaced with lower paid part-time ones. State aid for women initiated projects has, therefore, come from a poisoned chalice. The cash flowing from this cup has been miserly and imposed constraints which have threatened many of the egalitarian ideals embodied in woman-centred community action.

Woman-centred community action focuses on gender as a central feature of collective action taking place in the community and promotes social change which will foster gender equality, reduce the invisibility of women, and emphasize the processes whereby interaction takes place as well as the outcomes being sought. It forms the basis of feminist community action (Dominelli, 1992).

Women have also sought state funding to consolidate their initiatives in the community and safeguard their autonomy and ways of working (Schreader, 1990). However, women's pressure on the state to augment their meagre resources has not produced results capable of sustaining women's autonomous activities in the community at either the levels needed by women or the organisational forms they require. Nonetheless, women have persisted in developing woman-centred provisions without state support, although inadequate funding has truncated their growth. As a result of feminist organising, there has been a proliferation of badly resourced community groups seeking to extend women's options in both employment and service provision during the past decade, for example, rape crisis centres, health groups, playschemes. These have addressed issues which have had low priority on the state's agenda, for example, male violence against women, child care; raised their public profile by redefining them as social issues rather than private woes; and created services which respond to women's needs as they have defined them (Dominelli, 1992). Additionally, these woman-centered resources have provided women with the space in which to meet and work with other women, define their own priorities, explore new ways of working together and discover feminist social action as a method of addressing their concerns. Although women's ultimate aim of eliminating gender inequality has been frustrated by the state's reluctant support of woman-centred initiatives, the impact of these activities on women themselves have been encouraging. Despite its precarious financial base, woman-centred community work has created vigourous organisations.

The problematic nature of the relationship between women and the state seems set to continue into the 1990s as policies pursued earlier bear fruit. Prime amongst these will be the loss of public services and amenities, a reduction in the number of permanent full-time community work jobs, and fewer community resources especially earmarked to meet women's specific needs as women.

Woman-centred community action, therefore, has to address a number of critical issues during the 1990s. These pivot fundamentally on its relationship with the state and cover eight major areas. These are listed below without any specific order:

● identifying and furthering women's agenda for social action;
● ensuring the autonomy of woman-centred activities;

- securing funding for women-centred provisions free from arbitrary state imposed constraints;
- establishing egalitarian working relationships in the workplace and at home;
- developing a non-oppressive relationship between the state, the community and women;
- promoting the development of egalitarian relationships between adults and children and women and men in both public and private life;
- eliminating gender oppression in all its forms; and
- tackling racism and other forms of oppression.

This chapter will examine these issues in the context of the evolving contradictory relationship that exists between women, community work and the state. It will not make predictions about how this contradiction will be resolved, but will focus on the tasks that confront women undertaking community work in the 1990s.

Relating to the State: the Past Shapes the Future
The work that feminist community workers will have to undertake during the 1990s will be shaped in large measure by the activities launched and trends established in the previous decade. Thus, the legacy of the 1980s is crucial to understanding the opportunities and dilemmas women community workers will have to face in the 1990s. During the 1980s, feminist community workers were busy developing woman-centred resources. These were resources created by women, for women and run by women in accordance with feminist theory and practice. These provisions included rape crisis centres, incest survivor groups, refuges, well-women clinics, women's health groups and various co-operative ventures which covered a range of activities from women's therapy centres to commercial publishing houses. These initiatives owed their existence, theory and practice to the aims and objectives of the Women's Movement and were located largely in the voluntary sector.

However, there were also feminist community workers in the statutory or state sector. These had been appointed by local authorities, particularly through their social services, education, recreation and leisure departments and other publicly funded bodies, for example, the Manpower Services Commission (MSC). The MSC was later superseded by the Training Agency which was in turn replaced by the Training and Enterprise Councils. These agencies also supported a range of community work developments as part of the job creation process being promoted by the government to massage the unemployment figures and ensure that the long-term (waged) unemployed (particularly its youthful segments) did not escape the injunctions imposed by waged labour discipline for long (Davies, 1986). Although these latter posts are the ones acknowledged as being in the state sector, I would argue the state also plays a substantial role in both voluntary and commercial sectors through funding arrangements and budgetary control mechanisms which set the parameters around which these can operate.

However, feminist community work developments were only tiny oases in the vast desert of patriarchy. Their financial existence was perilous and their success depended to a large extent on the energies of women and the scarce resources they could squeeze from the state and extend through their energy, commitment and time. The concessions women wrung from the state meant the creation of a number of facilities not previously available to women. But, the price women paid for state support was high. State financing had a number of deleterious drawbacks to the independent development of women's resources and monetary value given to work women carried out in such groups. The obstacles in question have centred largely on the difficulties state imposed constraints have placed on a project's existence and its internal operations. The constraints affected the following areas of project activity:

a. accountability;
b. viability;
c. procedures of operation; and
d. recruitment of personnel.

In other words, state resources have been used to sculpt both the shape of feminist projects and the processes driving them. The state has exercised control over projects through fiscal mechanisms and inhibited their growth as feminist community organisations in the process.

Budgetary control becomes ideological control
State financing of projects is subject to fiscal restraints and budgetary procedures which ideologically inform budgetary practices and project evaluations in terms of a cost-effectiveness model which pays scant attention to a project's democratising objectives, the psychological benefits and socialisation opportunities women derive from group activities and the value they place on these. I shall now consider the impact of such budgetary control.

Being held accountable by the state for the finances it contributes to projects is a legitimate demand given their use of public resources. However, what is unacceptable is the limitations on collective action which state forms of accountability impose on women's groups (Ng, 1988). These restrictions are primarily oriented to meeting the needs of the state bureaucracy and indicate that those formulating these lines and methods of accountability have little sympathy for the more egalitarian and collective methods of working espoused by feminist groups. Responding to the ultimatums and timetables set by bureaucratic accountability, has distorted the aims and objectives which women have identified as being essential in their work (Ng, 1988). For example, women's groups seeking state funding might be required to designate a person in charge of the organisation, when the group's aims are to ensure that all its members share leadership responsibilities and reach decisions collectively. Ng (1988) graphically describes the impact state funding had on a black women's group addressing the needs of immigrant (sic) women. The tensions of having to respond to state dictat, impose hierarchical lines of accountability on collective group processes to secure funding ultimately led to the demise of the group. Consequently, a marginalised group of women rarely featuring in the government's list of priorities was denied a crucial resource.

In seeking state funding, women have sought to open up opportunities for securing economic resources in a context free from unequal gender relationships and the dependency these hoist upon women. While reliance on the state for financing has the advantage of offsetting dependency relationships which are directly negotiated between closely related individuals enmeshed in the unequal power nexus of the family, this move has not placed women on an egalitarian footing in financial transactions. The state apparatus is still controlled by white men who make the decisions about the allocation of resources (Howe, 1986; Dominelli, 1991; Walton, 1975; Ellis, 1989) and determine the forms of accountability which are deemed acceptable to a bureaucratic organisation which disburses funds (Ng, 1988; Ng, Walker and Muller, 1990). So feminist community workers still find themselves conducting negotiations with men who show little understanding of or commitment to their aims and objectives.

The criteria the state uses in deciding which projects it will fund have also had a crucial impact on a project's existence and its viability. These limits have been particularly important with regards to projects which the state has refused to fund or sought to curtail because it has regarded them as 'political'. As a result, these conditions have had a differentiating impact in that projects critical of the status quo or government policy are more likely to fall foul of the criteria adopted and be unfunded, than those projects not posing such challenges (Ellis, 1989). Ellis' (1989) experience has revealed that proposals with a feminist orientation, particularly those initiated by black women, run a higher risk of being excluded. Projects are also deemed non-viable because they are considered politically suspect, therefore, unreliable and unacceptable. Local authority withdrawal of funding from projects aimed at responding to the expressed needs of lesbian women in a number of London boroughs and the closure of several Women's Units in the mid-1980s are indicative of feminist community work activities being at the cutting edge of this politically inspired process.

Ironically, in Britain, the diminution of community resources at the disposal of the community worker to meet the specific needs of women as women in the 1980s was occurring at the same time as the country's highest political office, the prime ministership, was held by a woman. The government's abolition of the Greater London Council and the metropolitan counties in the middle of the decade seriously undermined woman-centred community work in general, but feminist community work in particular. This trend was exacerbated by the political swing to the Right, even in Labour held authorities where women's community work projects were amongst the first to be chopped when rate-capping exercises and public expenditure cuts took their toll (Whitlock, 1987).

The size of project being launched is also dependent on the state's willingness to fund women's groups (Dominelli and McLeod, 1989). Feminist projects seeking state funding might succeed in obtaining partial funding for their activities. For example, women's centres have obtained state monies for counselling or services responding to individual women's emotional needs because these are considered 'safe' whilst direct action or campaigning activities are labelled political and unfundable. But, partial funding means that the initial proposal has to be scaled down to the resources available. The skewing of the services offered to women attending Well-Women Clinics (WWC) illustrates the limitations in service delivery imposed by partial state funding (Foster, 1989). WWCs have been unable to provide the full range of services envisaged by women practitioners and users because of state funding restrictions. Additionally, the government's refusal to fund the outreach activities planned by those working in and using WWCs has meant that work aimed at improving services for working class and black women and increasing their accessibility to health resources has not been carried out (Foster, 1989). As a result, WWCs have been unable to develop as originally conceived in the women's health movement, though they have succeeded in providing some women with badly needed community based health resources. Funding is, therefore, critical in determining the viability of projects and whether services will exist in practice.

The constraints imposed by funding also affect group dynamics, processes and procedures of operation, that is, the ways in which those involved in a project work and promote their group interests together. Responding to the criteria set out in funding applications has created a hierarchical division of labour — anathema to feminist theory and practice — in feminist groups. Feminists have sought to transcend hierarchies imposed by funding considerations in their practice with varying degrees of success. For example, one of these hierarchies stems from the division between paid and unpaid workers where volunteers are used to undertake work which has failed to attract funding. This particular hierarchy can mitigate against endeavours aimed at ensuring the egalitarian treatment of and involvement in decision making at the point of delivery for all workers and users. In the case of the WWCs, many of the unpaid workers are volunteers whose knowledge of health issues is acquired painstakingly through training sessions and the work they undertake within the WWC. But, even in the areas of their competence, users tend to assign less weight to the advice of volunteers than to those uttered by qualified doctors paid by the NHS (Foster, 1989).

The recruitment of paid personnel for project work is also highly dependent on funding. Not only are the numbers which can be recruited affected by the funding which can be secured, but the type of worker appointed can also be determined by financial considerations. If money is earmarked for a particular kind of worker, it cannot be used for another, even though the work of the unfunded worker may be more essential from the point of view of the women workers and users. For example, funding arrangements have made it is easier for women to seek psychological counselling and support through the NHS than to obtain the services of a feminist counsellor or therapist working from a Women's Community Resource Centre (McLeod, 1987). Budgetary control, which is presented as a neutral and technical intervention in project activity becomes in practice, a highly political and ideological instrument of social control.

Feminists have constantly challenged the state's priorities in these matters through direct action aimed at opposing closures and the withdrawal of much needed amenities (Whitlock, 1987). But, in the context of a countrywide shift to the Right, a growth in the respectability accorded to familialist ideology, few successes have been forthcoming. Unfortunately for women, as the state's cost cutting operations and concern to support traditional family values moved into high gear, even less politically explosive provisions, for example, publicly funded nursery places, were drastically reduced. Women's failure to alter the state's stance has demoralised many women community activists, particularly those engaging in high profile community activities such as the Women's Peace Movement, Women Against Pit Closures, and caused the Women's Movement as a whole to become more inward looking and throw women into a more personalised, lower profile work which focussed on their own specific needs, gave rise to identity politics, and sought to make women's groups even more self-sufficient by relying more thoroughly on the resources they could extract from within their own ranks (Segal, 1987).

This reaction has impacted on feminist community work's relationships with the state and within its own organisations. Externally, in relation to the state, women's withdrawal from high profile community action has enabled the state to avoid having to take responsibility for tackling gender inequality in service provisions, including those provided under its own auspices. Institutional sexism remains endemic in state structures as a result. The rise of a new anti-feminist ideology that claims there is no longer any need for feminism as women have achieved equality and society is in its post-feminist stage, despite the glaring inequalities that exist between men and women, has further demoralised women activists. Women still constitute the bulk of society's poor, the wage gap between men's and women's wages continues to widen, women's limited reproductive rights are constantly being attacked, and women carry on doing most of the domestic work (Segal, 1987).

Internally, within women's own organisations, feminists have sought ways of addressing the myriad social divisions that divide women themselves, e.g., 'race', age, disability, sexual orientation, in a more realistic manner and sought to develop forms of practice which would respond to their new insights. This has meant the questioning and reconsideration of important nostrums, e.g., 'sisterhood is universal'. Through the process of critical self-appraisal, the complexity of women's oppression on a global scale has become more clearly understood. Sisterhood has become appreciated as something that has to be worked for, not assumed (Lorde, 1984). Besides leading to changes in local group practice, this realisation has also had the effect of broadening women's perspective on the international dimension, enabling women to re-evaluate it and take it more seriously. The Women's Peace Movement, the creation of networks amongst of European feminists and other feminist organisations are products of such revaluations.

Looking into the 1990s
The fragmentation of feminist community work activities in the 1980s remains a problem for community workers to address during this decade. Feminist community work's failure to obtain firmly grounded support at the heart of the political process in both the central state and its local variant is a serious shortcoming that requires urgent resolution. However, I am not convinced that tackling this issue through the formation of a women's political party and entering the electoral process is the way forward. At least, the Icelandic experience, where such an approach has been attempted has not yielded the results feminists desired (Dominelli and Jonsdottir, 1989). Indeed, some would argue that in Iceland at least, feminist initiatives have been thwarted and diverted from their purpose of ending gender oppression as existing political parties have rushed to include women's issues on their agendas in piecemeal fashion and the state has co-opted feminist energies into its own institutions and processes (Jonsdottir, 1991).

The same outcome seems to have occurred in Canada without a women's party. There, feminists employed by the state in various government quangos such as the Commission on the Status of Women and other local state bodies to respond to women's organised demands through community initiatives, have realised that their efforts have had little impact on the institutionalised forms of sexism perpetuated by the state itself (Schreader, 1990). The failure to achieve macro-oriented changes through community action suggests that more detailed and painstaking work needs to be carried out for feminist perspectives to: infuse the whole of society; affect individuals in ways they can personally comprehend; overturn institutional roles which legitimate and perpetuate sexist attitudes, behaviours and policies; and challenge the cultural norms which obscure the mantle of authority being used to cover sexist values and belief systems.

Whilst carrying on campaigning and consciousness-raising work on myriad levels, feminist community workers need to simultaneously maintain their work in the community, support women in their demands and promote initiatives aimed at redressing gender inequality. In the absence of adequate state resourcing, women need to continue creating appropriate services for women despite the financial famine conditioning their existence by drawing on their own talents and capabilities. Within this work, feminist community workers need to maintain their critique of state supported initiatives, particularly those which are predicated on the assumption that women have nothing to do with their lives except care for others. For without this critique, the state is lulled into perceiving women's demands for full equality as narrow sectional interests which can be responded to in marginalised ways without structural change, through limited forms of social engineering which confirm the status quo. Moreover, women have to continue demanding that children's rights be recognised and that the forms of masculinity currently lauded by society be exposed for the pernicious impact they have on the well-being of children, women and men themselves when they dare admit it (see Bowl, 1985; and Brittan, 1989 for further discussion of this point).

Sexism, Racism and Community Work: a Central Issue for the 1990s
Gender as an issue received scant attention in recent community work practice until women started demanding that the implications of gender inequality be examined in community work processes and its employment practices (Remfry, 1979; Dominelli, 1990). The same can be said of 'race'. Racial oppression was identified as a serious issue in the community work literature, when two black men, Ashok Ohri and Basil Manning, wrote the first extensive book, *Community Work and Racism*, on the subject back in 1982. Although it remains the most exhaustive analysis of the topic, it said little about black women's experience of gender in community work practice, and left a gap that remains to be filled.

The interface between gender oppression and racial oppression is a difficult one to unpack. Community work practice is no different from other areas of practice in this respect. Addressing this issue is not helped by the fact that racism remains a marginal issue for most community workers (Ohri *et al*, 1982), although a few have sought to intervene positively to change the situation (Thomas, 1986). Open, frank discussions acknowledging the fears white people have in working with black people and the fears that black people have about being at the receiving end of white racism have been possible for some workers (Ellis, 1989). But when it comes to improving practice in relation to black women, particularly Muslim Asian women, the problems white community workers have in providing anti-racist practice are compounded by the interaction between sexism and racism. They find it easier to respond to difficulties centring around language issues than they do to those involving understanding cultures, traditions, customs, religion and women's rights. As a result, Asian women and girls find very few resources specifically earmarked for them (Ellis, 1989). Or, if some facilities are provided, these tend to be marginalised, short-term projects with limited prospects for either project continuity or the careers of the Asian women staffing them because they are funded through Section 11 (of the 1967 Local Government Act), job creation schemes and other short-term funding arrangements.

Additionally, there is the question of who are the appropriate people for community workers to work with in matters involving Asian women and girls. White community workers tend to consult traditional leaders without thinking about the gender implications of doing so. Whilst this approach may be appropriate in some situations, it may not be in others. The male dominated traditional leadership may have been given this status by white people rather than its arising from Asian people's wishes (Yurval Davies, 1992), so their authority may be dubious. Such approaches also by-pass organisations which have been established by Asian women themselves and risk exacerbating gender divisions amongst Asians by ignoring the gender politics which are already evolving in Asian communities. Women against Fundamentalism, for example, have argued against the automatic assumptions made by white community workers that the only leaders in black communities are men (Yurval Davis, 1992). Stereotypical responses by white community workers can set back anti-racist struggles concerned with establishing gender equality and advancing the position of black women and compound the difficulties that need to be resolved. Additionally, white community workers' interventions may endanger the political affiliations and balance of power which Asian communities have created to resolve conflicts amongst themselves.

The interplay between sexism and racism poses complexities for black women community workers. Ellis (1989) describes the distancing an Asian woman community worker experienced when she was trying to convince the Asian male leaders in Cleveland that she was doing legitimate work with Asian women, even though her style was non-confrontational. There was a job of building up trust across various layers of the community she was working in before she could undertake action which it would endorse.

If the issue of establishing credibility is difficult enough for an Asian woman who shares many characteristics with the women she aspires to work with, it is immeasurably more difficult for white women to establish their credentials in this arena. Their views on what is appropriate action may not coincide with those of the Asian women they wish to work with. Sometimes, for example, Asian women may be willing to form a group for social or educational purposes without wishing to become involved in collective action. Their right to form a multiplicity of groups covering a range of different purposes must be acknowledged by white feminist community workers. A full evaluation of the community workers' position, the contribution they can make to the development of anti-racist community work in furthering the interests of particular communities and how this does or does not mesh in with the aspirations of the Asian women they want to work with needs to take place before they embark on action within a community.

An issue highlighting the need to weigh up all the relevant factors is domestic violence. Asian women have the right to consider how they want to handle this matter themselves. White women must learn to support Asian women's struggles on their terms, ensure that they address the issue of white racism in refuges that currently cater primarily for white women, the police force, criminal justice system, immigration control and other institutions that are brought into play in handling this issue (Mama, 1989).

At the same time, white community workers need to be aware of the complexity of community politics in Asian communities. Ellis (1989) describes how one Asian woman community worker had great difficulty getting some Asian men to accept her role as a community worker because she had previously supported battered women by working in a refuge. Supporting a black woman community worker in this context requires a deep understanding of Asian community politics as well as gender politics. White community workers are advised to resist the temptation to jump in to help on the basis of a superficial awareness of the issues. Being fully informed, a key community work skill, is even more important when working along anti-racist and anti-sexist lines.

Additionally, white community workers need to be aware of the enormous pressures on black community workers at all times to perform perfectly at all levels, including being the expert on all black people, not just the particular religious or ethnic group of which they are part, and the deskilling process which black workers are subjected to as a result of the inordinate demands white organisations place upon them (Ohri and Manning, 1982).

Finally, it is important to recognise that gender is as important an issue when working with men as it is when working with women. Yet gender is rarely considered relevant when working primarily with men or on issues which are deemed to have a more general 'community' relevance. White community workers often assume that gender bonding can operate across the racial divide and enable white men to interact unproblematically with black men. However, although gender may unite them, it can be virtually impossible for white men community workers to penetrate the sphere of Asian male politics without a lot of spadework to establish credibility and trust being undertaken first. Ellis (1989) describes how poor community work practice confounded the resolution of the dispute around single sex education for Muslim girls in Manchester because gender politics were ignored. In other words, being aware of gender politics is important for both black and white community workers, whether black or white, male or female. Although there are occasions when it is easier for white women to work with groups of Asian women, white community workers should not assume that Asian men cannot work with Asian women. Ellis (1989) highlights a number of issues on which sensitive Asian men work appropriately with Asian women's groups.

In working with black communities, some of the conflicts endemic to community work, particularly state funded community work, become sharpened. Illustrative of this problem is the question of loyalties, particularly for black community workers working for the local state. The state as employer expects organisational loyalty to its aims and objectives from its employees. But community work has a built in tension that asks community workers to identify to a considerable extent with the interests of the communities or groups they are working with as part of the job. This contradiction is inherent in community work because community workers have been set the task of raising awareness of and demands for services whilst at the same time not being given adequate resources with which to respond. This tension is exacerbated at a time of austerity, severe rationing, and corporate management — an uncomfortable reality of the 1990s. For black workers, the problem of conflicting loyalties is magnified by white fears that black workers will overidentify with black communities and endorse demands which the state is unlikely to support (Rooney, 1987).

In this context, the state plays a critical role in setting up community workers to fail, both in terms of their relationship with the communities they are trying to organise and with their employer, who can deem their activities as enough of a thorn in the side to discontinue funding the project, and/or dismiss the workers. These pressures have caused community workers in both statutory and voluntary sectors to assume more moderate, reformist aims in their work in the past few years (Butcher, 1992) following community organisational aims or moving away from field based organising and more into research, evaluation and training. Unless the economic situation improves these realities will become more central to practice rather than less. Women and black people will lose out in direct service provision at the local level as resources get diverted elsewhere.

Conclusion
Community workers must take gender politics seriously in the 1990s

if they are to respond to the agendas women — black and white — have set. A key feature of this process will be addressing the contradictory relationship between women, community work and the state and ensuring that it starts shifting in favour of women's liberation and gender equality. To facilitate the realisation of this objective, feminist perspectives and action must permeate all levels of society — the personal/individual; organisational/institutional; and the cultural/normative. Additionally, all community workers must ensure that those feminist community work activities that do exist are publicised and given a higher media profile. They prefigure the more egalitarian forms of social relations necessary in society as a whole. In short, working for structural changes enhancing people's well-being and personal growth must be at the top of community work's priorities for the 1990s.

References

Baldock, J and Ungerson, C (1991) 'What d'ya want if you don' want money? A feminist critique of 'paid volunteering' in Women's Issues in *Social Policy*, edited by M Maclean and D Groves. London: Routledge.

Bowl, R (1985) *The Changing Nature of Masculinity*, Norwich: UEA Social Work Monograph.

Brittan, A (1989) *Masculinity and Power*. Oxford: Blackwell.

Butcher, H (1992) 'Community Work: Current Realities, Contemporary Trends' in *Changing Social Work and Welfare*, edited by Carter, P., Jeffs, T. and Smith, M. Buckingham: Open University Press.

Carter, P, Jeffs, T and Smith, M (eds) (1992) *Changing Social Work and Welfare* Buckingham: Open University Press.

Curno, A, Lamming, A, Leach, L, Stiles, J, Ward, V, Wright, A and Ziff, T (1982) *Women in Collective Action*. London: Association of Community Workers.

Davies, B (1986) *The State We're In*. Buckingham: Open University.

Dixon, G, Johnson, C, Leigh, S and Turnbull, N (1982) 'Feminist Perspectives and Practice' in *Community Work and the State* edited by Crai, G., Derricourt, N. and Loney, M. London: Routledge and Kegan Paul.

Dobash, R and Dobash, R (1992) *Women, Violence and Social Change*. London: Routledge.

Dominelli, L (1988) *Anti-Racist Social Work*. London: Macmillan.

Dominelli, L (1990) *Women and Community Action*. London: Venture Press.

Dominelli, L (1991) '"Race" and Gender in Social Work' in *The Sociology of Social Work* edited by Martin Davies. London: Routledge.

Dominelli, L (1992) 'More than a Method: Feminist Social Work in Practice' in *Critical Feminisms* edited by K Campbell. Buckingham: Open University.

Dominelli, L and Jonsdottir, G (1988) 'Feminist Political Organisation in Iceland' in *Feminist Review*. No.27, Summer.

Dominelli, L and McLeod, E (1989) *Feminist Social Work*. London: Macmillan.

Ellis, J (1989) *Breaking New Ground: Community Development with Asian Communities*. London: Bedford Press.

Finch, J (1984) 'Community Care: Developing Non-Sexist Alternatives' in *Critical Social Policy*, Issue 9, Spring pp.6-18.

Foster, P (1989) 'Improving the Doctor-Patient Relationship: A Feminist Perspective' in the *Journal of Social Policy*. Vol.18, Part 3, July, pp.337-362.

Francis, D and Henderson, P (1992) *Working with Rural Communities*. London: BASW/Macmillan.

Gamarnikov, E, Morgan, D, Purvis, J and Taylorson, D (eds) (1983) *The Public and the Private*. London: Heineman.

Hanmer, J and Statham, D (1989) *Women and Social Work: Towards a Woman-Centred Practice*. London: BASW/Macmillan.

Howe, D (1986) 'The Segregation of Women and their Work in the Personal Social Services' in *Critical Social Policy*, 15, pp.21-35.

Jonsdottir, G (1991) Personal communication with author.

Langan, M and Day, L (1992) *Women, Oppression and Social Work: Issues in Anti-Discriminatory Practice*. London: Routledge.

Lorde, A (1984). *Sister Outsider*. New York: The Crossing Press.

Mama, A (1989) *The Hidden Struggle: Statutory and Voluntary Responses to Violence Against Black Women in the Home*. London: London Race and Housing Unit.

Mayo, M (ed) (1977) *Women in the Community*. London: Routledge and Kegan Paul.

McLeod, E (1987). 'Women's Experience of Love: The Significance of Feminist Therapy'. Unpublished paper.

Ng, R (1988) *The Politics of Community Services: Immigrant Women, Class and the State*. Toronto: Garamond Press.

Ng, R, Walker, G and Muller, J (eds) (1990) *Community Organisation and the Canadian State*. Toronto: Garamond Press.

Ohri, A and Manning, B., Curno, P. (1982) *Racism and Community Work*. London: Routledge and Kegan Paul.

Remfry, P (1979) 'North Tyneside Community Development Project' in *The Journal of Community Development*, 14(3). pp.186-189.

Rooney, B (1989) *Resistance and Change*. Liverpool: Liverpool University.

Schreader, A (1990) 'The State funded Women's Movement: A Case of Two Political Agendas' in *Community Organisation and the Canadian State*. Toronto: Garamond Press.

Segal, L (1987) *Is the Future Female? Troubled Thoughts on Contemporary Feminism*. London: Virago.

Thomas, D. N. (1986) *White Bolts, Black Locks: Participation in the Inner City*. London: Allen and Unwin.

Walton, R (1975) *Women in Social Work*. London: Routledge and Kegan Paul.

Whitlock, M (1987) 'Five more Years of Desolation' in *Spare Rib*, No.180, July, p.15.

Wilson, E (1977) *Women and the Welfare State*. London: Tavistock.

Worcester, N and Whatley, M (1988) 'The Selling of Women's Health Centres: The Response of the Women's Health Movement' in *Women, Health and Reproduction* edited by H Rosser. London: Routledge and Kegan Paul.

Yurval Davis, (1992) 'Fundamentalism, Multiculturalism and Women in Britain' in 'Race', Culture and Difference. London: Sage/Open University, pp.278-292.

6

Feminist Work and Community Education

Viv Rogers

The concept of community education is subject to similar confusions of identity as the concept of 'community' itself. It purports to be a lifelong learning process for people of all ages in adult education, youth work and community development. It professes commitment to meeting the needs of the whole 'community'. However, it lacks the necessary resources to do either of these, even if it were possible or desirable. In Devon, community education has peripheral status within education as a whole, and is therefore subject to arbitrary cuts in funding. Since the 1988 Education Act, community education in Devon has come under increasing pressure to define and justify itself — a difficult task when the service itself is not clear about its own aims and objectives. Without such clarity it fails to address the inequalities experienced by over half the population: women.

Feminist approaches to community work (Barker, 1986) and the position of women in adult education (Thompson, 1983) have been the subject of debate amongst women, and sometimes within academic institutions. But whilst senior managers in community education may pay occasional lip service to the needs of female staff and 'users', in general, attitudes to work with women vary from the paternalistic to the hostile, and feminist practice in particular is still marginalised or considered ineffectual, inappropriate or hysterical over-reaction.

It may seem surprising, and certainly frustrating, that in the 1990s the question of gender relations still needs to be raised and debated. There is a suspicion amongst many practitioners that this is mere nitpicking on the part of feminists. After all, equality is a reality, isn't it? Surely, especially at a time of squeezed budgets and threats to local government, we should get on with the business of working in our 'patches' with our own 'community' interests? The issues of housing, welfare benefits, dependents' care and so on cannot be tackled by community education workers anyway, and therefore it is important to concentrate on responding to the demands of consumers and funding bodies, and simply provide adult education classes and youth activities which offer vocational or recreational opportunities.

These positions are common within community education and ignore institutional sexism, and the horizontal and vertical segregation of work and its relative importance. The inclusiveness of women in the poorest sectors of society (Jordan and Waine, 1986/7), and the search for an authentic identity for both men and women which liberates rather than further oppresses, should suggest a continual re-examination of the values upon which community education is based, and the need for critical reflection on these.

Women workers in community education tend to be concentrated in lower status positions. Women commonly work as part-time paid or unpaid community and youth workers, propping up a system which could not exist without them, yet which often ignores their needs and barely acknowledges their existence in terms of value. Managers still tend to be mainly men, and even where they are women, they are often unsupported and may reflect the dominant views of the organisation and reinforce specific sets of power relations. Here as elsewhere, women who 'succeed' face a dilemma: whether to support the existing power structure or to work to change it from within. In either case, unlike men in similar positions, they are seen as representatives of their sex.

Those with whom we work, the 'users' of community education, are often defined by age or differing ability as well as by conventional notions of adult education and youth work 'provision', rather than placing adult and youth work in a community context. The framework for these debates lies in pluralist views of society in which community development has been the ideological meeting ground of the New Right, and of reformist conceptions of need within a model of defusing conflict and denying the validity of critical thinking. Community work becomes further identified as a palliative to increased central control (despite the rhetoric of locally-devolved power) with the worker as 'honest broker' between local people and agencies.

Gender, as a specific set of relations in which power is vested in an authentic concept of authority that is male, disappears, and is replaced by the needs of the economy for 'responsible' citizenship and for retraining.

The fragmentation of many women's lives (Hughes and Kennedy, 1985) and the daily juggling of various 'roles', their structural poverty (Scott, 1984), perceptions of their sexuality and sexual orientation, the position of Black women particularly in the 'white highlands'

of areas like the South West, is reflected in and reinforced by government legislation since the 1980s. This includes:
– the British Nationality Act, and the consequent oppression of black women 'dependents';
– the Social Security Act, particularly pernicious for women, and more than twenty changes to benefit regulations since 1979;
– the 'actively seeking work' test which discriminates against women in particular;
– Section 28 of the Local Government Act;
– Poll Tax inequality particularly 'joint and several liability'.
– the Child Support Act, and its coercion of women, particularly those on low incomes.

Community education does have a responsibility to recognise and act upon the social and political situation in which the vast majority of its 'users' — women — are found, and in which many more are made invisible by its failure to understand discrimination. It is at the expense of the women we work with that community education workers, particularly male managers, have become highly professionalised.

Part of the struggle to give greater clarity to the work is to examine and debate what community education objectives should be, and to evaluate actual practice in the light of these, and the values on which they are based. These objectives might be broadly defined as:
– a 'valuing' approach to people;
– challenging existing attitudes and knowledge;
– clarity of purpose;
– empowerment and ownership;
– training, and the personal development of paid and unpaid workers; and
– the generation of resources.*

In talking of values and principles, workers quite often mystify what is meant. There is also often a 'common language', shared by opposed political standpoints; for example, 'empowerment' can be used to mean either liberation, growth and awareness, or 'consumer choice'. So it is important to be explicit about the values from which we practice towards the objectives we have defined.

One of the initiatives in which I have been involved is a two-year course for women called 'For Our Own Good', which offers the opportunity for a flexible approach to 'learning'. This is organised by Wider Opportunities for Women (WOW), a Plymouth-based

---

*Acknowledgements to the others in the group who worked on producing this set of objectives at a community education conference: Jonathan Hyams, Dave Schwartz, Christine Smith, Tanny Stobart, Jeanette Stoneman, Jeff Stratton, Sharon Tappin, Sue Tate.

voluntary organisation (no direct relation to other WOWs), which has no paid workers, and which is run by women for women. The course is ongoing, and is designed to enable participants during the first year to engage at any point in the three subject areas: literature, history/herstory, and sociology. It examines women's writing, recovering the history of working class and Black women's lives, analyses gender relations in western industrial society, places these in a context which values and reflects on personal experience, and builds confidence to develop ideas further.

The second year aims to encourage women to present their ideas for discussion and to write these up in a project which is assessed through constructive criticism rather than graded marks. Childcare is free, the sessions are timetabled to allow for the picking-up of school-age children, and there is a nominal weekly fee, thus recognising the lack of financial independence for many women.

The course was planned and written in partnership with women involved in WOW's informal discussion groups. It brought together women from a variety of educational institutions, and took account of the needs highlighted at one-off workshops and media phone-ins. Over the short time that WOW had been in existence in Plymouth it had become apparent that women wanted a less formal route to higher education than was currently available through 'Access', or felt a need to increase their job opportunities, or wanted to spend longer looking at particular issues. There was lively debate about the need for a certificate at the end of the course, strongly argued for by those intending to participate. Through negotiation over a period of time with the University of Plymouth and the College of St. Mark and St. John in Plymouth, 'For Our Own Good' is now recognised as recent relevant study experience for entrance to one of their social science or humanities higher education courses.

Starting with the women that WOW already had contact with, participants were originally drawn from Plymouth and district through posters, leaflets and press releases. Four years on, contact is largely through word of mouth. There is no restriction on age. The only requirement is that of reading the course material. Women are supported in developing literacy, numeracy and oral skills within the structure of the course, as well as through formal one-to-one contact with facilitators.

The style of facilitating is not that of 'experts' teaching. It encourages participants to recognise their own knowledge, to look at how women have been de-skilled in a wide variety of contexts (not least in the educational packaging of 'traditional' female crafts), and to support a mutual exploration of feminist critiques. The gaining of confidence for women is not measurable within standard monitoring and evaluation procedures.

For some women, to work through a process of transition from low self-worth to greater assertiveness over their lives means being able to listen, to speak, and to see with a new awareness of the possibilities opened up. How can this be validated in conventional terms? It can be quite daunting to begin an undertaking such as this.

> I came in quite nervously at first. I thought it was going to be a lot of heavy stuff, but once that pressure was off, it gave me the confidence to question more. After years as a housewife you get out of the habit of expressing yourself. (Marie)

Working in a group can be harrowing.

> The thought of everyone looking at me made me crumble inwardly. (Linda)

There are also haunting experiences of school to overcome.

> You're quite afraid of doing things, putting things down on paper. But once I got down to it, I realised that it wasn't going to come back with things on it that make your confidence go, whereas at school, spelling and things were the most important things. (Yvonne)

An informal approach, however, can feel unstructured.

> I had my doubts whether this relaxed style of learning was working, it was so far removed from school . . . (Yvonne)

But feeling more confident is often mentioned by participants as important.

> Taking part in this course has awakened my brain and encouraged me to like myself, which in turn has given me the confidence to go out in the career world and get what I want. (Linda)

Being a women-only course is supportive.

> It's allowed me to grab time for myself as a person. It's very important that you can come into a group that hasn't got men in it. They tend to put you down and you can't seem to get out of it. (Yvonne)

Small group work has long been the practice of feminist organising, for consciousness-raising and for specific issues such as health. It offers the opportunity for participation on the basis of mutual equality and respect. Resistance to this form of work is often couched in funding terms: the 'bums on seats' approach still predominates, especially at a time of educational cutbacks. We need further research to examine ways of evaluating the richness and diversity of this potential and of making workers accountable to such groups.

Women's Studies and Access courses have proliferated over the last few years, and the WOW course can be seen as living within an academic acknowledgement and validation of the prior learning experiences of mature students. This is based on some acceptance that it is possible for learning to relate to everyday life and still be critical and reflective. Whilst this may well require systematised learning opportunities such as those offered on Access courses, their formality can provide yet another hoop for students to jump through rather than being a genuine attempt to challenge academic traditions of acceptable and legitimate education. Humphries (1988) has cogently argued for a re-evaluation of the liberalism of values upon which adult education is based and which merely serves to legitimate existing inequality.

The explicit framework for the WOW course has more in common with a community work 'empowerment' approach than with the liberal academic tradition or New Right economic 'functionalism'. But it is essentially an educational process, one that actively engages with women's lives in a dialogical relationship based on Freire's conceptions of liberation as opposed to domestication and further social control (Freire, 1972, 1985).

The ideas behind this educational process are not new. A recognition of the position for women in schools (Spender and Sarah, 1980; Lees, 1986) and ways of changing this (Brah and Deem, 1986); in the family (Barnett and McIntosh, 1982); in lesbian relationships (Campbell, 1982); their invisibility in history (Spender, 1988), and what they have to say in their writings (Woolf, 1977), share a collective voice reflected in the actions of women in their local communities (Curno *et al*, 1982), as well as acknowledging differences (Phillips, 1987). Women are and have been in struggle, in acting upon their real situations and trying to change them. The reflectivity necessary to the Freirean model of dialectical change can be embodied in courses like WOW's. There are no assumptions of solidary 'sisterhood', but a valuing approach which starts with women's own experiences and ideas, and allows the critical space in a small group setting to gain the confidence to reflect on and develop these. Anti-discriminatory practice means that through a rigorous critique of a variety of feminist themes, a more authentic identity as women can be worked towards for both participants and facilitators.

Challenging dominant views of gender, 'race' and class stereotyping becomes possible once women feel more personally confident. Gramsci's twin conceptualisations of 'civil' and 'political' society are useful in this context, as O'Brien (1986) has argued. A mediation between the culture of 'civil' society, as expressed within some notion of familial relationships, and economic reality maintains consensual political thought and actions. However, critical consciousness in the form of 'education' can bring about the breakdown and transformation of such cultural hegemony. The personal and political can be integrated into an understanding of the need to challenge, and can generate change.

Whilst Gramsci's analysis has limited use for women, as his conception of universal 'man' stemmed from a male supremacist position as does the bulk of 'codified knowledge' (Spender, 1981), nevertheless its clarity has much that can be learned by any educational endeavour.

Clarity of purpose does not mean slavish adherence to a set of values which bear no relation to people's lived reality. As Rowbotham (1985: 211) says, we need 'a culture which you can tug and shape with complexity'. It does however rely on acknowledging that while we work within definitional priorities, these are rarely made explicit. If we are not clear about anti-discriminatory principles, we reinforce the dependency of particular groups on dominant and established views. Working with any group in feminist praxis should be co-operative, involving a shared and negotiated process of 'action and reflection'.

This intense learning experience does not just happen though. For women on the WOW course and for the workers involved as facilitators it is important that, as elsewhere, there is a sense of ownership about the learning that takes place, and this can be worked towards through a Freirean belief in the need to 'existentialise philosophy' and 'philosophise experience' (Kirkwood and Kirkwood, 1989: 136).

Women talk about their own learning positively.

> At the beginning it's like being switched on, like a light bulb. Then after that it's what we do ourselves within the group. And it goes on and on! (Linda)

Education has been seen as liberating and a way out of poverty (Bryan *et al*, 1985). But in order to get at the meaning of experiences

> we need to reflect, to compare them with other (similar *and* different) experiences and to do so we need to use existing concepts and insights, as well as helping to create new ones. (Kirkwood and Kirkwood, 1989: 135)

Not only do we need to validate existing experience, we also need vision about what is possible, rather than merely reproducing present power relations. Uncovering women's history and studying the contexts of class and culture differences is an important part of helping to construct an alternative framework.

Participatory training in anti-discriminatory principles and practice is one strand of the construction of this debate and lives within feminist and community work praxis. Local authorities and voluntary organisations rely on central funding for training. Central funding sources reflect New Right ideologies of individualism, thus dispossessing large sections of society. Community education could, as Cowburn has argued,

> become the method for unlocking the talents, skills and abilities in those whom education has derided, mocked and patronised for well over a century. (Cowburn, 1988:27)

This means sharing available resources with groups in examination of similarities and differences in perceptions of needs; a complex and difficult task when there are so many varied views of the world. Quality training for workers, paid and unpaid, needs to be accorded a higher priority. With anti-discriminatory training, management committees could make more sense of aspects of community education work which do not attempt to be all things to all people.

Green (1989) has argued that such participatory training increases the effectiveness of managers, workers and local groups as they are involved in a process of analysis, reflection and evaluation of resources that exist within the community. It also gives the potential to look at perceptions, attitudes and actions and the implications these have for their own lives and development as well as for the lives and development of others in the wider community.

A strategy for developing access opportunities has been explored by Cowperthwaite *et al* (1989). Four stages of a process are identified:
● individual action in changing attitudes to learners through training;
● institutional action involving a review of the internal organisation;
● allocation of extra resources to priority areas of work;
● and wider policy and curricular action through the rigorous application of equal opportunities policies and action.

However, we might argue that whilst positive action for recruitment of more female managers, responsive assessment criteria and accountability procedures are important, it is not a *sufficient* condition for changing current orthodoxy about learning choices, particularly for women. There is also resistance by organisations to change. But it would be refreshing to see a real commitment to such action, backed up by codes of practice and effective grievance procedures!

Making alliances where possible on parts of the work which share common values, and acknowledging where they do not, can be productive and can help harness scarce funds and generate other resources. WOW works in partnership with individuals and with voluntary and statutory organisations. For example, Community Education workers facilitate the course sessions. WOW attempts to inform the practice of other agencies over particular educational issues which effect women, dependents' care being just one. We still need to work at whatever level we can with other organisations and groups who might support our aims and objectives in particular areas of work. This conclusion of Rowbotham *et al* in the late 1970s (Rowbotham, Segal and Wainwright, 1979) is no less pertinent in the 1990s to get us beyond the fragmentation of important issue-based work.

One continuing problem for informal groups and courses like WOW's is that they usually exist in isolation from other educational initiatives and institutions which remain unresponsive to need. So, for example, should women wish to pursue a higher education course, not only may the approach to learning be different, but structural barriers may prevent access in the form of lack of dependent-care, inappropriate timing, and so on. Support to overcome this is often lacking. But there also needs to be a synthesis between different learning opportunities so that a course like WOW's is only one of a varied range of options that women may choose for themselves.

A reflective participatory style of work is not a luxury. It is an essential component of a way of reaching out to women's experiences and knowledge, and of developing confidence in these. Feminist practice is rich and effective work in the 'practical and cultural reductionism' (Flynn *et al*, 1986:140) of the present political climate. It offers much that can provide adult and youth work in the community with a set of values upon which to work towards anti-discriminatory practice. It can present coherent and consistent arguments for the centrality of the work, rather than patriarchal models which seek to colonise the work or ignore it as irrelevant.

The proposed objectives of community education stated earlier and the choices these allow for expression and development of experiential learning have particular relevance for feminist work. Once clearly articulated, the objectives can be used to look at evaluating practice, in the *value* for people of educational opportunities, and they can offer a way of being accountable to the groups with whom we work. As a process of empowerment the collective and critical principles of feminist organising should be complementary to and enhance the various projects within community education, thematically informing the theory and practice. However, what has tended to happen is that a series of ad hoc responses to tightening financial control at the local level, uncertainty whether community education has a future within current educational restructuring, and hegemonic control by the centre of the language and culture of the 'consumer' has cast adrift any serious attempt at being clear about the diversity of needs, and therefore the opportunities, for women as a social group.

It is hard to construct alternative debates in a political, economic and social climate which discourages critical analysis. The struggle for greater clarity and effectiveness in challenging oppression and holding out a vision of how things could be is often derided by those who hold power. It becomes demoralising for individuals to continue in these circumstances. But the alternatives must be constructed if community education is to be anything other than a vocational and recreational 'service', largely irrelevant to those whose access to opportunities is limited by poverty, and whose lives are most sharply affected by discriminatory policies and attitudes.

References

Barker, H. (1986) 'Recapturing sisterhood: a critical look at "process" in feminist organising and community work', *Critical Social Policy*, Summer.
Barrett, M. & McIntosh, M. (1982) *The Anti-Social Family*, Verso Editions.
Brah, A. & Deem, R. (1986) 'Towards anti-sexist and anti-racist schooling', *Critical Social Policy*, Summer.
Bryan, B., Dadzie, S. & Scafe, S. (1985) *The Heart of the Race*, Virago Press.
Campbell, B (1982) 'A Feminist Sexual Politics: Now You See It, Now You Don't', in M.Evans (ed) *The Woman Question*, Fontana.
Cowburn, W. (1988) 'The Coming Crisis of Community Education', *Journal of Community Education*, Vol.6, No.4.
Cowperthwaite, P., Johnson, R. & Ryves, M. (1989) *Access in Action*, NIACE/REPLAN, October.
Curno, A. *et al* (eds) (1982) *Women in Collective Action*, Association of Community Workers.
Flynn, P. *et al* (eds) (1986) *You're Learning All The Time*, Spokesman.
Freire, P. (1972) *Pedagogy of the Oppressed*, Penguin.
Freire, P. (1985) *The Politics of Education*, Macmillan.
Green, J. (1989) 'Education, Training and Community Work', Final Year Dissertation (unpublished), Polytechnic South West, Plymouth.
Hughes, M. & Kennedy, M. (1985) *New Futures Changing Women's Education*, Routledge and Kegan Paul.
Humphries, B. (1988) 'Adult learning in social work education: towards liberation or domestication?', *Critical Social Policy*, Autumn.
Jordon, L. & Waine, B. (1986/7) 'Women's income in and out of employment', *Critical Social Policy*, Winter.
Kirkwood, G. & Kirkwood, C. (1989) *Living Adult Education*, Open University Press.

Lees, S. (1986) *Losing Out*, Hutchinson.

O'Brien, M. (1986) 'Hegemony and Superstructure: A Feminist Critique of Neo-Marxism', in R.Hamilton and M.Barrett (eds) *The Politics of Diversity*, Virago Press.

Phillips, A. (1987) *Divided Loyalties*, Virago Press.

Rowbotham, S. (1985) 'Revolt in Roundhay' in L.Heron (ed) *Truth Dare or Promise*, Virago Press.

Rowbotham, S., Segal, L. & Wainwright, H. (1979) *Beyond the Fragments*, Merlin Press.

Scott, H. (1984) *Working your way to the bottom: the feminization of poverty*, Pandora Press.

Spender, D. (ed) (1981) *Men's Studies Modified*, Pergamon Press.

Spender, D. (1988) *Women of Ideas*, Pandora Press.

Spender, D. & Sarah, E. (eds) (1980) *Learning to Lose: sexism and education*, The Women's Press,

Thompson, J. (1983) 'Women and Adult Education' in M.Tight (ed), *Opportunities for Adult Education*, Croom Helm.

Woolf, V. (1977) *A Room of One's Own*, Grafton Books.

7

Mapping the Community Work Minefield

Working in an Unpredictable Arena

Nick Derricourt and Jennifer Dale

In his famous treatise 'On War', Clausewitz says many things that could be considered seriously by those seeking to contrive more peaceful strategies. He writes that it is very hard for anyone who has not personally experienced war to understand why it is so difficult and why a commander should need exceptional ability.

> Everything looks simple; the knowledge required does not look remarkable, the strategic options are so obvious . . . Everything in war is very simple, but the simplest thing is difficult. (Clausewitz, 1976; 119)

The main reason why it is so difficult is that so many things can go wrong.

> Countless minor incidents — the kind you can never really foresee — combine to lower the general level of performance, so that one always falls far short of the intended goal. (*ibid*; 121)

The 'force that makes the apparently easy so difficult', he calls 'friction'. He explains that

> the·good general must know friction in order to overcome it wherever possible, and in order not to set a standard of achievement in his operations which this very friction makes impossible. (*ibid*; 120).

No one who has worked in community work for any length of time will need to be reminded that 'the simplest thing is difficult'; in fact it is a highly unpredictable business subject to that very same friction that makes war so difficult to wage.

The 'war of position'[1] in which community workers with any socialist aspirations in the 1990s are engaged, is a grinding one, and, we would suggest, subject to the same difficulties. In the 1980s, community work, never simple, became a very difficult thing to do.

The local authorities, whose policies and practices community workers have sought to change, themselves laboured under a loss of control to the centre. The populations with which community workers have sought to work have been under intense pressure from increasingly residualist social welfare policies. So where opportunities to do community work have arisen, the circumstances have usually been very difficult ones, fraught with obstacles and unpredictabilities. Working in such conditions has required a clarity and discipline which has been very demanding of community workers, who have to keep track of a lot of factors and issues, not all of which are fully recognisable at the outset of a programme or even after some time. A crucial part of the community work exercise is struggling for clarity about what is going on, who one's allies are at any given point, who are neutral and who are antipathetic, and why. All this has to be tackled in a situation which is usually changing all the time; people can be friendly to start with, and become hostile or more neutral or vice versa. Moreover, participants are often friendly (or at least neutral) about some aspects of community work, but antipathetic about others. Part of the skill of community work is finding and working with that part of people that is well-disposed. Finding hand-holds is an essential skill.

Nowhere are these qualities more urgently called for than in the area of alliance making. Alliance making occupies a position of central importance for those community workers who are interested in helping to keep the door to socialism open. By helping 'ordinary' people to work together to maintain services and commodities that are still in a qualified form in community or public ownership, community work can give them confidence to press for it. This involves helping people to feel good about finding ways of co-operating with others to work in this direction, and to help them to feel good about representing and getting resources for others. In short, it means helping to keep alive people's sense of their own and others' right to a decent life. Although *Beyond the Fragments* (1979) appeared some years ago, the problems and possibilities remain much the same. In particular, the opposition to capitalism is as fragmented as ever. In the struggle to defend and improve public sector housing (with which this chapter is concerned), tenants are often fragmented; fragmentation also accurately describes the relationships which persist between tenants and the housing staff that are supposed to serve them.

It is hard to see how community work can make any worthwhile progress at all without working on alliances, since community work's resources are so modest. Sometimes these alliances will be made for reasons that are not the same on both sides, as when two diverse agendas overlap or complement each other. Moreover, alliances are often volatile, formed and dissolved over a matter of weeks, or even suddenly disrupted, so that one needs to be alive to the ever-present possibility of shifts.

This was made very clear in Rochdale where we conducted an evaluation of a community work project from June 1985 to February 1988. During this period, we observed 42 relevant meetings together and separately, interviewed key participants and informants (140 interviews), and examined a large number of relevant records and documents. Our purpose was to produce a full qualitative assessment of the process of the project at both management and community level. We pooled data and cross-checked where we could. In the course of this work we confronted problems about evaluating community work. Evaluation of community work cannot sensibly be linear; broad agency objectives are turned into detailed agenda in negotiation between the community workers and residents. Such agenda emerge and are often reshaped according to changing circumstances. With this in mind, we began to envisage the project, the estate, the other agencies which were servicing it and working there, and other main participants, as an arena in which agreements about objectives were negotiated and renegotiated as a result of the interactions that took place between people and agencies. So part of our evaluation procedure took the form of talking with people who could tell us how that interaction worked, how objectives were shaped and re-shaped, and how constructive they thought the process was. To help us to do this, we gradually developed the idea of a matrix which enabled us to plot the agenda of participants and the way they perceived the agenda of others. We explain what we mean by matrix in more detail later in this chapter.

Why Rochdale?
The Community Project Foundation (CPF) asked us to evaluate their project, and we agreed to do it because there seemed to be relatively favourable circumstances for conducting a piece of 'classic' community development which might actually be successful. In fact the problems that arose in the Rochdale project were very instructive, and so was the success that was achieved. We believe that the problems are typical enough of community work to be worth sharing with a wider audience.

First, we should explain the background to the project. Rochdale Community Project (RCP) was set up in 1981 by Community Projects Foundation (CPF), a national voluntary organisation funded by central government, with joint funding from Rochdale Metropolitan

Borough Council. RCP was accountable to CPF and advised by a management committee which involved CPF, local authority officers, representatives of the local co-ordinating body for the voluntary sector, and RCP's project director. In practice, the project director had considerable operational independence.

The original agreement described RCP's role as being to develop residents' organisations in community based action areas (CBAAs), which were areas of older, privately owned housing, targeted for area based improvement. The administration of the CBAAs was devolved to area based offices responsible to a section of the planning department. The relationship between the RCP's project director and his department was characterised by the borough planning officer as the 'arm's length approach', whereby community work should be broadly helpful to the local authority, yet within a framework of independence which could tolerate a degree of tension.

Towards the end of 1983, the borough housing officer, who chaired the RCP management committee, began to express interest in the idea of RCP extending its work to council housing estates. He was impressed by what had happened in CBAAs and saw it as a model for developing a more productive relationship between his department and its tenants. He believed that tenants suffered from ignorance as to how the system worked, but recognised that housing officers could not educate tenants without being paternalistic. So community work had a key role in developing tenants' skills and understanding of the local government system. At the same time the housing department needed to devolve responsibility for a local budget to estate sub-committees to make participation worthwhile for all concerned.

The estate chosen was the borough's largest council housing estate, consisting of 2,288 dwellings (flats and houses) of traditional design, built mainly in the 1940s and 1950s. In the early 1980s it had a range of problems. The dwellings had suffered from poor maintenance in the past, and the repairs service was very poor. Most of the houses had unmodernised kitchens and many were damp. Despite the suburban layout, tenants complained that the estate looked awful and felt demoralised by the amount of rubbish and litter. The estate had a high level of domestic burglary and tenants felt that it had a bad name. The estate was widely perceived by both tenants and officers as consisting of 'good' and 'bad' areas. A high percentage of current lettings were to young single people and single parents, who were housed alongside an often long established population of middle aged and elderly people. Many older tenants felt strongly that the estate had "gone down".

The estate had a tenants' association (TA), which had been in existence with one break for over 20 years. It was described both by officers and other tenants as being ineffectual. Its monthly open meetings were heavily dependent on the willingness of the area housing manager to attend and run a kind of surgery for tenants' complaints.

The estate was administered by an estate based area office, which was also responsible for two other estates. Facilities at the office were cramped and staff felt under considerable pressure. There were numerous complaints from tenants about how they were treated by officers — who in turn believed that they were having to take the brunt of tenants' anger for things that weren't their fault.

By the summer of 1984, the borough housing officer and RCP's project director had completed negotiations, and in November 1984, two community workers began work based in a flat in the centre of the estate. At this point, we would like to introduce the *dramatis personae* as at the beginning of the project.

The borough housing officer (BHO) played a key role in bringing RCP onto the estate. In 1984, he appeared to have a good grasp of community development principles and argued that it needed to remain independent in order to avoid becoming part of the 'defensive apparatus of the department'. He was in agreement with the workers' aim of trying to develop groups who could put their case effectively to the local authority. He clearly believed this as a matter of principle and as part of his vision of 'adult-adult' relationships between officers and tenants.[2] He also hoped this would be to his benefit in putting pressure on other more powerful departments such as Architect's and Engineer's.

The assistant borough housing officer (ABHO) was not particularly sympathetic to community work, and professed himself slightly bemused about its aims and how its achievements could be measured. He was initially pessimistic about the possibility that resources might be secured for the estate, and feared that the project would put misplaced pressure and an additional workload on the housing department staff especially at area level. As the area housing manager's line manager, he was a key figure, although he seems to have been the housing officer with whom RCP had least contact.

The area housing manager (AHM) had not been involved in the decision to involve the community project on his estate. He had the largest area and largest number of area staff in the borough to manage. The office was very busy and cramped. The AHM felt that he was being asked to run more and more experiments in his area without a sufficient increase in staff. Seemingly all at once, there had arrived in his area an estate sub-committee, which was supposed to be taking over estate budgeting some time in the future, a Department of the Environment Priority Estate Project (PEP), and a community development project which he had not been consulted about, with more in the pipeline. He too had professed himself unsure of what community work was. He had been used to a relationship with a TA which was dependent on his department, and worked closely with it. When the TA carried out a repairs survey in the early 1980s, they acknowledged the help of the housing office, and used the office as a return point. So his expectation had been that the new community project would be a direct help to him — for example in doing the door knocking for tenant consultation. He too was worried about the pressure of work and feared that more groups would mean a proliferation of meetings for him.

There were three councillors, two Labour, of whom one lived on the estate, and a Conservative. All were active, but it was the two Labour members that the project had most to do with. One of them was Labour's housing spokesman and widely tipped to become the chair of the housing committee should Labour take control at the May 1986 elections. He became from the outset quite closely involved with the project. The other Labour councillor lived on the estate, and had been secretary of the tenants' association from 1979 to 1981. He still kept in touch with some of the committee members from that time, although he had a very poor opinion of the current chairman (who was a Liberal). He was hoping to be re-elected to the ward in May 1986.

The tenants association (TA) began with mixed feelings about the project. At the beginning, some members were quite welcoming on the grounds that they could not cope alone with such a large estate, and that they could use help in preparing for the sub committee meetings. Others were less sure whether the project was needed. Their doubts began to take the shape of fears that the project was in some sense intruding on 'their' patch.

The community workers did not know how long they would be working on the estate full time. They knew it was a very large estate to do community work on, but because of the support which they understood was available to the project from the borough housing manager, they expected the housing department to have an understanding of the 'arm's length approach', and to be committed to tenant consultation and participation. This meant that they expected the AHM and a yet to be appointed Project Development Officer (see below) to be receptive to the work of any groups that they might help to form, and co-operate with them in the provision of information required by such groups.

Two other categories of *dramatis personae* were not there at the start of the project, but appeared on the scene soon after. Firstly, there were the members of the 'new groups' ie., those helped into existence by the community workers. The first group, Dampfree Kirkholt (DFK), was formed of a nucleus of TA members, who were then joined by 'new' tenants who had shown an interest in the issue of dampness at street-based meetings. The second group, the Kirkholt Repairs Improvement Group (KRIG), was set up after the street meetings, and included both TA members and 'new' tenants from the beginning.

Secondly, there was the Project Development Officer (PDO), who was appointed in relation to the PEP after the community project had been established. Although she did not think that she had been given a very clear idea of the role of the community project, her job description suggested a wide-ranging, innovative brief outside the duties of day-to-day housing management. She took a little while to settle into her new job, since she had to continue spending time at her old one in a housing aid centre until a replacement there was appointed.

The Matrix as a Tool in Research
Our task was to evaluate the project. We thought we could best do this by trying to understand the implications of the original objectives and by examining how working objectives emerged and were modified in the interactions that took place between the several participants. As we have said above, our attempts to study the interaction suggested that it would be useful to envisage an arena in which a complex web of inter-action was played out over time. This arena can best be represented by a matrix. The term matrix can be used to denote a diagram in which a web of interactions or relationships can be plotted and examined. We used the matrix as a research tool in our evaluation, because we were able to plot on it and scrutinise the actions of each participant. In this way a very full and dynamic picture could be built up of what was going on, how the work developed, how the participants' expectations, agenda, communications, misunderstandings, difficulties, goals, interests, ideas, opportunities, alliances, and sources of danger shifted over time and in relation to changes that were going on in the whole arena.[3] Of course, the arena is not a closed system. Events and changes which took place outside the arena affected participants and interaction within it; we were able to plot these on the matrix too. What we now wish to suggest is that the matrix is not just a useful tool for evaluators (who, as we did, came in from outside to spend time with the project), but is

also an extremely useful tool for workers and their supervisors. Community workers do work in highly complex and unpredictable situations; to make sense of such situations, they need a device that will be thorough and sensitive to shifts in agenda, alliances and all the other things we have already mentioned.

The Use of the Matrix in Community Work
We are suggesting that a matrix is needed to detect and map these opportunities and shifts; by this means each relationship and agenda is studied carefully. The exercise can be begun at the start of the project, and done regularly throughout the life of the project. It can, of course, be particularly useful at times when problems arise. It may be useful if we spell out the steps that one needs to take when developing and using the matrix. The first step is to identify and note the key participants. They can be properly depicted in a matrix (see Figure 1).

The matrix could of course be more complicated, but if all conceivable participants were included, it would become unwieldy. It is probably better to keep it to no more than ten participants. When you are clear who should be included in the matrix, take a felt tip pen, and a large piece of paper and make a diagram (like Figure 1) which shows the key participants. It can of course be rejigged to include others when particular issues need to be examined, and it can of course also be used occasionally to examine a particular set of interactions about a specific issue.

The second step is to try to gain an understanding of the agenda of each participant. Take each person in turn and write down next to their place on the matrix (or, if you prefer, on a separate piece of paper) what their agenda is, using such questions as: what are they supposed to be doing? What are they trying to do? How do you see what they are trying to do? What is hindering them from doing it? What beliefs do they have and what pressures are being exerted on them? Then, from the position of each of the participants in turn, note what you can about how you, as that person, view each of the other participants in turn. If you don't know the answer to any of the questions you put to yourself, or do not know how you as that person view any of the other participants, make a note of it for later. It will probably be worth finding out. Be as imaginative as you can. It is actually quite surprising how much you can tell about how people see the world by putting yourself in their skin. Take your time over the exercise, and make notes of any ideas that it prompts as you go along. It both takes and develops clarity of thought, creativity and empathy. It can be made quite playful by doing it with other people, whether supervisor or colleagues, particularly if

Figure 1.

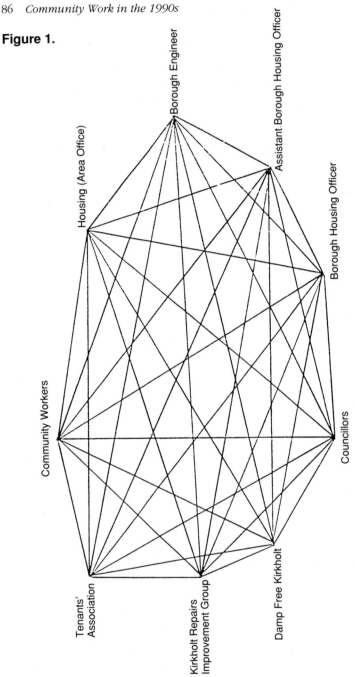

Borough Engineer

Assistant Borough Housing Officer

Housing (Area Office)

Borough Housing Officer

Community Workers

Councillors

Tenants' Association

Kirkholt Repairs Improvement Group

Damp Free Kirkholt

one uses role play or simulation techniques. Of course, it can be done on one's own, but then it is better to work at it in short blocks of time.

After doing this exercise, you should have a good picture of the arena in which you are working, and be able to identify where the other participants have a complementary agenda. This will help you think more clearly about the chances of constructing alliances. One would expect it to be easier to construct alliances with those parties who share the same goals, but of course, working successfully together doesn't just depend on that. For example, all the participants may agree that a particular problem needs putting right, but may have different perceptions of who is responsible for the current state of things. People can easily be alienated if they think they are being unfairly blamed for problems which are not their fault. Participants will of course vary in the extent to which they can handle apparent criticism. Some may relish a little gentle sparring whilst others may react defensively. Assumptions about how officers or tenants 'should' react may work in some situations and be wide of the mark in others. People may also feel upset and demoralised if they are not given due credit for the time and effort they are putting into trying to change things. This can be particularly complicated where credit is given to some participants and not others, or where a rival group is seen to claim credit unfairly.

These are just some examples of the many process problems which can cause alliances to falter or break down. Can the use of the matrix help to avoid some of these pitfalls? With the best will in the world, some alliances don't work, but we are claiming here that you can use the matrix to help you through the minefield. We offer the following four reasons to support this claim.

Firstly, if you have looked at each participant's agenda as thoroughly as possible, you should have an idea of how each sees the problems of the estate and whose responsibility it is. You can then do your homework and check out if you think they are right. If you find that you agree with them, you may be able, for example, to help a group to avoid unfairly blaming the wrong person. Knee-jerk reactions, which can lead to self-fulfilling prophecies (like assuming all officers are 'bad' because they are officers), can be avoided. On the other hand, if you find you disagree, then you can make a more realistic assessment of the possibilities for a successful alliance.

Secondly, if you have really tried to 'get under the other person's skin', you will have seen things through their eyes, and this will help you to predict how they will react. For example, in Rochdale, the AHM felt very overloaded with work; he had not been consulted about the decision to set up the community project; he wasn't sure what community workers were supposed to do; his line manager did not really think community work represented value for money. We could perhaps predict that he would not be very receptive to the community project.

Thirdly, you may not be able to solve the problem on your own; you may have to involve other people in your agency and in the local authority. Developing the matrix will give you more confidence in demonstrating to them that such problems have to be taken seriously.

Fourthly, being forewarned does not make the problem go away. But it does help you avoid being taken by surprise when relationships don't develop as you hoped. Alliances undoubtedly come under strain because of unpredictable events, which are bound to happen in the course of a community work project (just as they do in a war of position). People die, leave, transfer their allegiances, get elected, have personal crises, have rows, and lots more. We would argue that if a community worker is equipped with a framework with which she or he can plot the likely effect of any occurrence, she or he will be better able to take the necessary steps to support the constructive developments in the programme.

For these reasons, we are suggesting that the matrix is a good way of plotting shifts of agenda systematically. To do this, you need to switch from seeing the matrix as a snapshot of the participants at the beginning of the project, to seeing it as a moving picture.

We do not have space here to show in great detail how the matrix can be used, so what follows will necessarily be short and incomplete. But we do hope that it will give readers some idea of the possibilities of looking at community work in this way. With this in view, we will now briefly demonstrate some of the ways in which the matrix can illuminate some of the problems that arose when community workers in the Rochdale project tried to work with tenants who wanted to improve their estate through engaging in a participatory process with the local housing department. The work involved some quite tricky problems of constructing alliances. We have already outlined the key participants. The workers had to tackle three potential sources of fragmentation: between the TA and the housing officers (local officers, area based officers, and senior management), between the TA and the 'new' tenants' groups, and between the project and the local councillors. We cannot here give a full account of the history of the project, so we shall take two examples to illuminate the issues. The first looks at some questions surrounding the construction of an alliance with the AHM around the matter of repairs. The second looks at the difficulties encountered in constructing an alliance between the TA and the 'new' tenants' groups. It also shows how the shifting basis of an alliance with one of the local councillors impinged upon this process.

KRIG was one of the new groups formed by tenants who wanted to get something done about the repairs service on the estate. Since officers at all levels in the housing department had also identified this as one of the main problems that needed tackling, there seemed to be a potential basis for an alliance between tenants and housing. On the other hand, this could not be assumed, since there were differing views as to who was to blame for the current problems, in particular, whose fault it was that there was such a backlog of uncompleted jobs. Housing officers were clear in their mind who was at fault: the borough engineer and his department, which was responsible for carrying out repairs. In their view, the inefficiency of his department put them in a position where they spent a lot of time fending off complaints about a service over which they had no control.

The borough engineer of course took a different view. According to him, the root of the problem was that housing didn't pay enough to secure a decent service. In addition, housing officers, who ordered the repairs, were abusing the system by overloading him with so-called 'emergency' repairs.

The community workers and KRIG clearly needed to work out where they stood on these two competing explanations. If the community workers' homework had confirmed that the area housing manager was broadly correct in his view, then there was clearly a good basis for working together to put pressure on the borough engineer and his department. This was likely to be strategically very important. The community workers were unlikely to make much headway on the estate without the cooperation of the AHM. However, it couldn't be taken for granted that he would be a sympathetic ally. Although the borough housing officer was committed to the idea of community work involvement on the estate, this hadn't percolated down through his department. As we have already mentioned, the AHM hadn't been consulted before the project was set up, and feared that it would cause him a lot more work. Finding an issue where he could see the project as broadly helpful might have significant long-term payoffs. On the other hand, if he felt that he were being put under unfair pressure, any negative feelings about the project would be reinforced.

KRIG in fact invited both the borough engineer and the area housing manager to separate meetings. KRIG handled the AHM a bit aggressively and he in turn did feel that he was grilled rather unfairly. This happened partly because KRIG hadn't clearly targeted the borough engineer as the problem, partly because KRIG was keen to establish itself as a force to be reckoned with, and partly because several tenants had had bad experiences of dealings with area office staff. Several felt resentful about off-hand, even rude, treatment they had had from housing officers, and this carried over into their attitude towards the AHM. It predisposed some to blame housing officers for the problems — for example, some tenants believed that housing officers often threw away repairs slips rather than sending them to the borough engineer's department.

There were no more two-way meetings between KRIG and the AHM, however, since the repairs issue was taken to a higher level working party involving officers (including the AHM from housing and a middle manager from engineer's) and KRIG. Relationships here proved constructive. KRIG members felt able to put their ideas forward, and officers seemed to take notice. KRIG took several officers to visit Islington to see the locality based repairs system there, and this seems to have had quite an impact on the borough engineer, who after revisiting Islington off his own bat, did implement many of the changes to the repairs service that KRIG had been seeking.

The borough housing officer did give KRIG a lot of credit for the borough engineer's change of heart. On the other hand, the AHM and the middle manager from engineer's saw it as much less significant. They tended to stress their own role, with KRIG acting as a useful support. This left KRIG feeling that they had not really got their fair share of the credit. The situation was made worse by the fact that the estate sub committee had been set up on the estate as the official forum for consultation between officers and tenants. For various reasons, the tenants' representatives were all drawn from the TA. All new initiatives on the estate were formally agreed at the sub-committee. Public acknowledgement for the new repairs experiment thus seemed to accrue to the officers and tenants on the sub-committee, leaving KRIG out. This meant that, although an alliance of sorts was eventually formed within the working party, this was not really explicitly acknowledged by the AHM, leading to a situation where KRIG enjoyed some undoubted 'success' but didn't end up feeling that it got the credit for it.

The second example highlights some problems of alliance making. We would like to start by posing the question: did the TA and the 'new groups' have to be at loggerheads? It often happens in community work that tenants' groups working in the same or adjacent territory become opposed to each other and come to symbolise the divisions in 'the community'. Can community workers use their skills to help community groups to work together and overcome the differences in their agenda? We would suggest that such differences often arise out of a sense of threat, on the grounds that people who are not sure of where they stand, make their stand more secure by differentiating themselves from others near them, even if the interests of those others are objectively not very different from their own.

The TA had been going for a long time, and saw itself as an established respectable body with good links with the area housing office, and, from the autumn of 1984, a formal role on the estate sub-committee. It did, however, seek to get jobs done and complaints put right by taking up individual issues with the Area Housing Office. There were individuals on the committee who saw themselves as able to take the AHM to task, but when it came to it, they were so reliant on his goodwill that they rarely felt able to give him a hard time.

KRIG sought to identify itself as an energetic group of people who took a dim view of the TA's record and insisted that they could take matters further. Their own uncertainty at the start of the project probably contributed to the likelihood that they would have to see themselves as different, separate, and to see the TA as a pale thing. The TA sent rather unfortunate representatives to KRIG, a move which students of group work literature might recognise.[4] The two TA representatives just did not fit in, and were perceived by KRIG members, with some justification, as being quite disruptive. KRIG did not kick them out; in fact, they put up with them, although some KRIG members drifted away, mainly, it appeared, because of the uneasiness which filled the air when the TA representatives were present. When the TA representatives decided that KRIG was not for them, and that they did not feel welcome, they left, and KRIG got going again. In the meantime, the community workers had been pursuing friendly relations with other TA committee members, who were much more "sensible" and who actively represented the TA on the estate sub committee. To return to the question: could KRIG and the TA have worked together, instead of working in different places with different styles? What could have altered the alliances, for the TA was drawn up with the AHM, and the KRIG and DFK were drawn up with the community workers, while the councillors and the BHO did not for most of the time align themselves once and for all with either side? The main shift occurred when the resident Labour councillor acted in a way which arguably had a marked effect on events and underlined the importance of monitoring the perspectives and agenda of councillors. After the TA's Liberal Chairman (whom the councillor strongly disliked) unexpectedly left the estate, the councillor began to take the side of the TA in the politics of the estate, loudly denouncing the 'new' groups as 'splinter groups', which strengthened the TA's view of itself as the representative body. So, while the departure of the Liberal chairman could not reasonably have been foreseen, when it happened it led to a chain of events which caused the workers and the project some problems which had to be engaged with. It is possible that monitoring the resident Labour councillor's agenda could have at least alerted the workers or the 'new' tenants to the possibility that the councillor would switch sides if the opportunity arose; they could then perhaps have softened his action, which might then not have had quite the critical impact that it did have.

Conclusion

Readers may say that we are offering these illustrations and coming up with ideas with the benefit of hindsight. This is perfectly true, but we are convinced that using the matrix can give workers insights into opportunities and risks as they go along. If the two experienced RCP workers in Rochdale did most things right, and enabled part of the project to be successful, but missed things which arguably turned out to be important (and surely it is utterly forgivable that they should, given the complex nature of the work), then less experienced workers need properly supportive frameworks to pick their ways through the unexpected things which are to be found in the constantly changing arenas in which community work is played out. In the course of this work we were able to observe community work in action and to see how successful community work depends upon tracking the agenda of key participants and determining possible alliances, shifts of loyalty, interest and meanings, in order to relate constructively to those participants and enable one's own constituency to make the best of its resources. Only if this is done carefully and persistently, we think, will it be possible for community workers to translate socialist objectives into anything that looks like a real gain.

Note

The authors are very grateful to the Nuffield Foundation for a grant which made possible the research on which this chapter is based, and to the Community Projects Foundation (now the Community Development Foundation) which also contributed funds to the work.

Some of the earlier pages of this chapter resemble material given in a shorter paper which appeared in the *Community Development Journal* (Vol.25, No.1, 1990, pp.64-74). We are grateful to the Editor of the *CDJ* for allowing us to draw on that article.

Footnotes

1. The phrase 'war of position' was used by Antonio Gramsci, the Italian Marxist, to denote the kind of struggle which he thought could be conducted in civil society by working class men and women when a 'frontal attack' on the State is impossible. See Hoare, Q. and Nowell Smith, G. (eds) (1971), *Selections from the Prison Notebooks of Antonio Gramsci*, Lawrence and Wishart, (p.206). Gramsci thought that the war of position is 'difficult and requires exceptional qualities of patience and inventiveness.' (p.239).

2. An 'adult to adult' relationship denotes one kind of interaction in the typology of interpersonal interactions developed by Eric Berne and named by him Transactional Analysis. (See his *Games People Play* and also Pitman, E. (1984), *Transactional Analysis for Social Workers and Counsellors*. Routledge Kegan Paul.)

3. The matrix was in fact developed as a research tool over the course of three years. Here we owe a lot to David Silverman's Action Frame of Reference, Silverman, D. (1970) *The Theory of Organisations*, Heinemann, (pp.126-146).

4. When one group is threatened by another, its response may well be 'fight or flight'. This response is characterised by irrationality and tends to promote to a leadership role the individual whose demands are felt to offer the opportunity for flight or aggression and who often has paranoid tendencies. (See Bion, W.R. (1961), *Experiments in Groups*, Tavistock).

References

Clausewitz, C. von (1976), *On War*, Princeton University.

Rowbotham, S., Segal, L., and Wainwright, H., (1979), *Beyond the Fragments: Feminism and the Making of Socialism*, Merlin.

8

Black Empowerment: Gaining Strengths and Setting Agendas

Haydae White

This chapter is dedicated to the memory of Phil Bashford, friend and personal tutor, who inspired me to seek racial and sexual equality in my work.

I believe that black people involved in community work can assist in the process of personal and community change by allowing themselves time to re-evaluate their practice, get to know themselves, find individual and group strengths, and then take control of agenda-setting for and by black communities. I have learned resilience through taking time out to gather my thoughts in consultancy, training and in black support groups. These forums have offered me an opportunity to rediscover and redefine who I am from a position of strength.

Some of my experiences have left me feeling as if my innocence and eagerness to be a good "black" worker, willing and able to use my skills with black peoples, has been somewhat abused. Many agencies claim commitment to equal opportunities but seem reluctant to move beyond the rhetoric of an equal opportunities policy statement. When I discovered I was not alone in my endeavours, I enlisted the assistance and support of other black workers and formed a black workers group, which proved to be an inspirational environment to develop skills and strategies, and to raise awareness.

Unfortunately, few black community workers are in environments that assist in their personal development as black people, unless they seek this in informal settings outside of the workplace such as community groups, training and black support groups. This evidently means that managerial responsibility for black staff is regularly offloaded onto informal forums that are marginalised arenas. In addition, these groups often lack any direct say in the decision-making of the institutions employing black workers. Although I do not agree with colluding with such a marginalised arrangement, I recognise that for some black community workers it is their only lifeline when working in and with white-dominated institutions.

Many black community workers are no longer convinced by the seductive language of equal opportunities alone. Neither are their communities. We have only to look back at positive examples in black history to demonstrate the energy that arises from an increasingly politicised and vocal black community, angry at being enslaved, angry at colonialisation experiences, and angry at receiving poor life chances. When black community workers are aware of their black history they are more likely to set agendas challenging their present situations. Black empowerment needs to benefit our many black communities of peoples of Asian and African descent. Lastly, although community work has been viewed as the radical footing for equality issues, sadly it can, on occasions, prove to be detrimental to black community development.

Bristol and Black Empowerers

Having worked in Bristol I found that like other cities in Britain, there are the usual factors of poverty and discrimination, particularly around the inner city. Both city and county policies attempt to address these issues through revitalisation and service development in the most deprived areas. However, some would argue that many cities are not responsive to the needs of the black population within its boundaries. The uprisings in the early 1980s demonstrated the frustrations of increasingly vocal black communities (along with white local people) who were angry at the reluctance of the city and county councils to act in consultation with black communities.

As a result of the uprisings, hasty piecemeal measures were taken which again angered black groups. The reason for this anger was that there had been little if any consultation with black people about what they wanted. Instead, major buildings were erected in St. Pauls, and funding for voluntary groups has poured in, seemingly with little long-term planning.

Many black community workers felt that the impact of the uprisings, and the anger at the city council's measures following the uprisings, gave further cause for fear amongst white-dominated community organisations. The council's resultant panic at wanting to be seen to address race equality in the white-dominated community work field was hurriedly to recruit black workers, often within unsuitable organisations. Some black workers felt that they had to develop their skills unsupervised, which could prove difficult if working with racist members of the community or with black communities anxious for access to scarce community resources. The black workers were often ill-equipped because they were not provided with supervision or a structured programme of training to develop their skills. It almost seemed as if the apparent gaps between white community work and black communities would magically disappear with the arrival of a black worker.

Some black workers said that recruitment and training were largely Eurocentric, middle class, white and lacking in black perspectives in their application. It meant that black people were unable to carry out their work effectively and were seen to have 'sold out' by black communities. Attempts to create black support groups were frowned upon by white staff/managers and course leaders. However, white only groups were unquestioned if they justified their existence by claiming to counteract racism.

In effect what actually happens is that committed black workers are recruited to ill-equipped organisations keen to tackle race equality and anti-racism but often lacking clear plans of action. When the black worker is employed they are expected to resolve the many demands of the diverse range of black groups — find solutions to racist practice in the organisation as well as provide good generalist practice with little support. This undoubtedly leads to a 'double burden' where black workers' agendas are set by the black communities they originate from and work with, as well as by the white workers' fears. The black workers have at least two jobs to deal with — that of community work, and that of the race expert offering advice, support, training, networks, counselling and campaigning. The potential for burn-out is inevitable if this situation is not recognised and halted (Albany 1988).

Having provided managerial and non-managerial input for black staff, I feel black workers need a supportive environment to recognise these commonly shared issues and to place them in a wider political and historical context. Hopefully, this will lead to a recognition of structured evaluation, supervision and advice to enable black workers to function more effectively within the challenging environment of community work.

These issues are by no means the exclusive experiences of black workers in Bristol. I have heard and seen similar issues in other community work and social work settings throughout the country. However, unlike many other areas where black people are in significant numbers, Bristol seems to lack the forums for black people to meet and gather strength. Training, consultancy and support groups are by no means the only solutions to the problems mentioned, but they could prove to be a small step in the right direction towards black empowerment for black workers.

Setting our own Agendas: Examples from Training
This section will provide a brief description of some of the work I have carried out in workshops, consultancy and conferences in Bristol to try and illustrate the beneficial effects of black people gathering to gain insight and strength.

I have run workshops for groups of black workers from the same setting or similar local organisations to enable them to debate their shared experiences and make sense of these. Before they can achieve the ultimate goal of developing strategies and strengths, I feel it useful for us to raise our shared awareness of ourselves as black community workers, placing this into a wider political, historical and localised context. From this I hope to expose our often hidden talents, recognise these, and possibly incorporate these strengths in a strategy that benefits us as black people. Initially what I did was to find out why participants were attending the workshops. To do this I asked them to describe themselves by mentioning significant facts about themselves. I then asked them why they were attending the workshop and, lastly, what they hoped to gain from attending.

Unlike running workshops for white participants, most black-only groups I have worked with generally refer to themselves in terms of their colour. In attending the course they aim to both tackle insensitive and demanding white-dominated institutions, and address the needs of neglected black communities that have had harsh experiences at the hands of statutory authorities such as the police, education, housing and social services. They were often willing to explore self-help options and voluntary community work alternatives to alleviate their situations. For some participants these apparent needs and demands on their time and energies proved to be ample motivation to reflect on their practice and future strategies at the workshops. One participant said that although her project had claimed publicly that they wished to create greater links with Asian communities, it had in effect left her without clear guidelines. Alongside this, the long-term work she undertook about her returning to Asian communities was dismissed as irrelevant. This worker felt betrayed by the management who had initially appeared to have public anti-racist sympathies. She wished to know how to cope with these situations in future. Another worker had been criticised for looking for new play resources in a centre which reflected positive black images. She was told that the budget was not sufficient to finance such an expansion. When she asked for a black consultant, she was told that she had to find someone from the existing collective, although none of the members were black. She refused and recruited another black worker to the collective who later became her consultant. She then experienced great verbal hostility from a white member of staff and was excluded from important decision making meetings. These examples are by no means unusual instances of the discriminatory behaviour meted out by fearful racist staff and management committee members in community organisations nationally.

At other times black workers have said that the more enlightened and committed white staff can also prove to be a hindrance, because of their often over-ambitious but unplanned approach to race equality. One black participant said she felt supported by her boss on a verbal level, but he often failed to recognise the significance of her work being blocked on numerous occasions. If, however, he did recognise and challenge the perpetrator directly and loudly this often made it difficult for her to work with the perpetrator. She also felt as if her power was taken from her by other white workers who were dealing with issues on her behalf rather than with her.

At the end of this feedback I asked them if they could clearly state what was wrong with the actions of their white colleagues apart from them making the black staff feel uncomfortable. The participants summarised that they felt powerless, the 'race' debate had now become a handy badge for subtle racists to hide behind but little action had resulted from the equal opportunities rhetoric. The black participants become increasingly drawn into making up for the inadequacies of a Eurocentric, outdated community work.

Another session involved looking at what made us into the black people of today. What experiences, what ways of operating made us *black* community workers rather than just community workers? The participants were able to provide numerous examples of shocking racist incidents from personal and work experiences which had made them "angry", "apathetic", "sad", "energised", "strong", "blacker than before", and "badly wanting change". They talked about being in unsupervised, unsympathetic agencies where they had to develop good practice on their own to meet the needs of the communities they served. They particularly felt that both black and white communities would find their work of more interest, because of their visibility at community forums. Then there was pressure to perform, and perform far better, than white colleagues.

Some participants were becoming rather depressed at the negative images they shared about their work and felt that there was little I could tell them to change their minds about the situation.

However, I conveyed my sympathy with their situation and shared my work and personal experiences with the group. We then looked at British history and what this can teach us about ourselves. We then brainstormed as much information as we knew about British history involving Asia, Africa and the West Indies. Few of the participants knew of the many positive contributions black people had made to Britain's culture, politics, health and education over hundreds of years. The only black history taught to the participants at school had focused on slavery, without mentioning the slave uprisings and organisations which made slavery uneconomic.

Many participants said they felt a lot prouder having heard this. History defines who you are by retracing where you have come from and if you are led to believe you only have a negative past, you will believe negative images about your present and future life. The group felt cheated of their history and were determined to find out more.

We looked at the history of race relations in Britain and definitions of racism to enable us to share a common understanding of this. We then looked at the skills and strengths we had as black people that were over and above what we are paid to do at work. At first, the group was hesitant to speak and giggled a great deal before one member said: "this is serious, we have an opportunity to look at this — we should answer honestly".

Reluctantly the group took it in turns to talk about their often unrecognised strengths. After each person spoke I asked the group to confirm if this was true, and if they felt the feedback was lacking that they should give positive feedback on the strengths the speaker had not mentioned. This session led to noticeable changes in the atmosphere in the room, and I certainly noticed the group members seeming to grow and smile.

All too often black community workers are set impossible tasks such as, "go forth and resolve all the issues for the black community" — without supervision, feedback or supportive forums.

Little time is provided to develop cross cultural/racial management techniques which allow black workers the space to feel safe and talk honestly about their work, their needs and their strengths. White institutions interact with black people and black institutions through fear rather than understanding. There needs to be a boundary setting and rules for interaction on a work level. Personal offloading is always unequal for black staff when faced with misunderstanding and the defensiveness of many white staff.

The last phase of this session I spent confirming how uplifting it was to be amongst such talented black workers; the future looked promising. But why did they continue to work for such agencies? I was met with a stunning silence.

We then moved onto recognising the areas of concerns within community work for black community workers and, of course, inevitably ended with an extensive list. After prioritising these we looked at identifying what was wrong, what should change and how should this be done. The last question was "what part are you prepared to play in this change as a black worker?"

Some participants said they should stand back far more often rather than always stepping in to bail out inadequate white agencies. Others felt they should be examining their white colleagues' practice and encouraging them to work more co-operatively on issues of racial discrimination and race equality. We looked at the stress of being a community worker, juggling diverse community needs, carrying and staying within the limitations of funding. These stresses alone make a community worker's life pressurised. But as a black worker you are expected to be a race expert, race counsellor, race trainer, race campaigner all without adequate management. The result is the 'double burden' syndrome. For this exercise I draw upon a flipchart and people brainstormed all the pressures of being a community worker around a matchstick figure. Underneath the figure with all the written responses I write 'STRESS' in capitals. I then draw another figure which is the black community worker and again ask for the participants to call out the pressures experienced by this worker and underneath these responses write 'STRESS x 2'. I give no feedback as the presentation alone is dramatic enough. The participants welcomed this as a reminder of their human limitations, without offloading the total responsibility for their principles on race equality.

We then looked at other long and short-term strategies, but we kept veering off on tangents because of the participants' feelings that the reception to their ideas would be negative. I asked them again,

"Why do you work for organisations which hinder your potential and in which you remain isolated and hurt although you have such positive strengths?"

I was met with silence for a while. Then one participant said "we assume we have to stay, but we could be doing things for ourselves".

I was due to run some follow-up sessions with this group but all have resigned from their jobs; two for re-training and one for another job. Those I spoke to felt liberated enough not to tolerate such an organisation and felt better equipped to challenge in future.

My consultancy has thrown up the same issues, but often isolated workers feel less able to attend forums elsewhere. However, when they do it seems beneficial in sharing experiences and developing strategies. I have also found that often a siege mentality occurs because of the distrust of white workers who verbally support black staff and then deny this later. These examples although dramatic highlight how black workers need to operate in a defensive arena of community work. Possibly it can be more effective to ask the "right" questions in order to preserve energy rather than offer answers as black workers whose skills and abilities are not acknowledged.

Further work carried out in at least three organisations began similarly in that the co-ordinators of the community organisations told me that the black staff would not meet with me. The reasons given were that the black staff did not see themselves as black. They wanted to integrate not separate, otherwise it might cause apartheid at the work setting, and so on.

When I actually set up times to meet with black staff I was never surprised. On the whole the majority of black staff attended and were very vocal in their concerns. On more than one occasion the shared 'black' experience debates I facilitated went on for over an hour longer than scheduled.

The questions I asked of the black staff looked generally at:
i)   the experiences of black staff within the organisation
ii) the perceptions of white colleagues' expectations of black staff
iii) their expectations of themselves.
iv) any perceived limitations due to the lack of management support.
v)   their positive strengths.
vi) training and support needs.
The answers were startlingly matched.

The black staff felt that although organisations may make grand claims, the reality is that there is either embarrassing hesitation to act, or a heavy handed intervention to stop black staff from gaining a group identity.

White staff could at best be sympathetic, but many acted as if the black staff who claimed to be victimised at work had asked for it. The accusation of 'you have a chip on your shoulder' was frequently forthcoming from white staff. At times, a divisive tactic had been to see black identity as so indefinable as to be redundant.

Some white staff had learned a great deal as a result of training and anti-racist management practices, but could often face victimisation if they rallied to support black staff within their organisation.

Many black staff had become increasingly politicised about their blackness because of the conflicting demands and differential treatment at work. Some mentioned feeling disillusioned with community work being equated with empowerment, because in their experience as black staff they had felt disempowered.

A lot of the black staff felt that making sense of the life experiences of being black in this country had been painful as well as liberating. It had also added greatly to their commitment to the many black communities, and the strategy for resolving black community needs.

I then looked at how I could facilitate change by working together with these staff to pressure management to address the needs of black staff and black communities.

The Values of Training and Consultancy

I do not imagine that the techniques I employ will be of value to all black community workers for all time, but I have found them useful, not without reservations, in my work as a trainer and lecturer. However, I do believe that training and consultancy for black community workers for black empowerment is valuable for several reasons.

1. It allows black workers to gain greater insight into their work, who they are, and the role they can and do play in the scheme of things.
2. Black workers sharing experiences also share strengths if allowed time and space to do so. This is not to say that all black groups are safe, enlightened groups, but they have the potential to be.
3. Black workers often of necessity have to develop good practice in their work because of the pressures on them to perform and consult in their work. However, few managers or committees are able to channel this talent without adequate support and training themselves.
4. Giving black workers the space to develop realisable goals prevents a situation of 'double burden' or burn-out. This time should be structured in as a regular evaluation of being a black community worker.

My reservations about the training I have done are:

1. These workshops are generally short-term, dependant on scarce sources of funding and generally are at the end of a long list of other training. There is no structured training for black community workers although the training they need will at some stage differ to that training given to white community workers.
2. Trainees and consultants like myself are not an integral part of the decision making structures these black workers return to. Our powers of management are therefore limited to mere suggestion and advice. We really need to see more sensitive black

community work managers as well as sensitive white managers.

3. White institutions need to recognise the importance of meeting the rights of black people otherwise they may vote with their feet or demonstrate in other ways. Many voluntary community work agencies rely on funding which in turn requires adherence to equal opportunities. How many agencies would be able to demonstrate this, I wonder?

In Conclusion

I feel that there is little I can add to the powerful and emotive topic of black empowerment. My techniques may have been basic, but they have powerfully unlocked the frustrations of black staff in predominantly white community organisations. To summarise:

1. People facing discrimination should be afforded the right to speak and be heard, even if there is disagreement with their views.

2. There should be justification about the way that white managers and colleagues respond to black staff, bearing in mind the equal opportunities/anti-discriminatory policies of community organisations.

3. Community work needs to move from a position of complacency around equality issues. The equality debate is dynamic, developing, stressful, educational and good practice backed up in law.

4. Joint agendas need to be set that respectfully address black and white staff's needs in a way that does not leave black staff cheated, because they are expected to be unpaid, unsupervised, unsupported race experts. If race expertise is sought, contracts and pay should be agreed with race advisers rather than informal race advice from colleagues.

5. White staff should undergo race equality training on an on-going basis, with black staff receiving on-going black empowerment/ support.

6. Black staff need to stop themselves from feeling as if they are solely responsible for redressing the balance in favour of race equality. Time out is needed to analyse and share common experiences and develop strategies where black workers set the agenda rather than follow other peoples' agendas.

References

Albany (1988). Video *Racism in Local Authorities.*

9

The Case for 'Rural' Community Work

George Giacinto Giarchi

A chocolate box image of country life sits incongruously upon the ugly realities of rural deprivation (McLaughlin, 1983). Images of cows in buttercup meadows, thatched whitewashed cottages and haystacks, abound. Romanticised and stereotypical descriptions of pastoral bliss and false assumptions of a closely knit community, nestled around the village green, block out any realistic understanding of what life is all about in rural settlements. However, there is another more insidious misrepresentation and myopic view of the countryside. It is created by those same social scientists who react against romanticised ideas about village and rural life and vigourously demythologise rurality.

As this chapter will demonstrate, the valid social science contention that there is no dichotomy between the urban and the rural, may have unintended consequences for community work practice in rural settings. Only when this is discussed can the identity and role of the rural community worker be adequately dealt with.

Few should question the commonality between urban and rural deprivation, because structurally each is determined by the same capitalist system. However, the repeated stress upon the structural does take away from the distinctive, qualitative and experiential aspects of rural life and their attendant problems. In socio-economic terms the city, the town, the village and the wide open countryside are inextricably inter-connected. However, in socio-psychological and anthropological terms, whatever the theoretical commonalities, the rural peoples' ways of life, orientations, expectations and problems are worlds apart from those of the urban people. In other words, their biographical 'life-worlds' are different. Indeed, the rural is not any one thing, it is a complex world of diversified settings punctuated by plural life-styles and multiple problems which are often *sui generis*.

If these factors are valid and community work is to be contextual, it follows that there is a significant difference between rural and urban community work, and that unquestionably there is a special case for *rural* community work. These considerations have serious implications, especially within the context of the community care strategy following upon the National Health Service and Community Care Act, 1990. There are enormous consequences also, for the way social policies are formulated; the way social and health services operate; the way community work courses and in-service training programmes are designed and taught.

Community work education must include within its learning packages the following three cardinal factors:

1. The rural world has distinctive features.
2. The rural world has endemic peripheral social problems.
3. The rural world has need of specialised community workers.

The chapter will then end by discussing the nature of rural community work.

The rural world has distinctive features

The mistake is often made of lumping realities under 'the countryside'. Russell (1986) states that there are in fact four countrysides:

1. the urban shadow countryside;
2. the accessible countryside;
3. the less accessible countryside;
4. the remote or marginal countryside.

This classification reflects to some extent that of Cloke and Edwards (1986), which ranges from extreme non-rural, to intermediate non-rural, intermediate rural and extreme rural.

The urban shadow countryside consists of the surrounding rural sprawl, just beyond the urban boundaries: often a mix of discontinuous suburbia and semi-rural settlement groupings. Here, the urban incomers, many of whom are commuters, often outnumber the well established rural households. Being near to urban areas, where services are centralised, the meeting places and service facilities tend to be minimal.

The accessible countryside lies beyond the shadow countryside, usually reached within an hour's travelling time by public transport from urban bus stops. Here the established rural households outnumber the urban incomers. Here, a mix of urban and rural issues characterise the local conversations at meeting places and in households. Here, there is often a noticeable unease between well established rural families and the urban incomers.

The less accessible countryside is unmistakably rural, characterised as it is by a low density population, loose networks of infrastructure and services, and a landscape dominated by farming and forestry, and often over an hour's journey by transport from high density urban areas. This is in line with Cloke's (1985, 1986) 'index of rurality'. A localised rural view of the world tends to over-arch everyday relationships, transactions and politics. This is part of process of 'cultural accounting' (Cohen, 1978): where the 'rural' is 'us': where the 'urban' (townies and city folk) is 'them'. A distancing takes place, which creates macro political divides between peripheries and centres. A distancing also creates micro barriers in minds, hearts and emotions, which are situationally unrelated to the urban scape and singularly related to the surrounding rural scape (Giarchi, 1984). Cohen(1982, 1983, 1987) has explored these pervasive phenomenological worlds. The divides are not created by hedgerows, woodland and grasslands, but by rural symbols and innuendos in everyday encounters. Not only is the countryside less accessible to urban people, so too are its folklore and vernacular values.

The remote or marginal countryside is the least populated. Here the villages are fewer; distances between those that do exist are greater; and households are least accessible. Well established rural families vastly outnumber the incomers. Political independence is highly prized and change is usually unwelcome.

The geographers such as Cherry (1976) and Dover (1980) identify land use as the significant rural factor. Cloke (1977) extends the Department of the Environment's (1971) use of three indices to sixteen, as a means of defining what is 'rural', which are based upon measurements of population, occupation, migration, housing and distance from urban centres. Cloke (1978) identifies the 'pressured' rural areas in which the urban creates the major influences/problems locally, eg. the demands of in-migrants and the impact of rural industrial change.

The sociological literature and economists have identified the trend towards the movement of large capital-intensive projects to rural areas, such as power stations — water and nuclear, and also oil terminals, and as in Scotland in the seventies, the concrete gravity structures (Giarchi 1984). These studies of counter-urbanisation have, in local rural areas, focused upon the mix and structural interplay between the urban and the rural economies, and the resultant culture clashes and impact of industrialisation upon the local way of life in experiential terms. The point to make is that the massive intrusions are exceptional and occur only in certain selected areas which are far outnumbered by Russell's countrysides.

Many anthropologists, particularly Cohen (1982) and Strathern (1982, 1984) have enabled the social scientist to appreciate the qualitative aspects of life in rural settings and the conflicts which result from counter-urbanisation. Recent anthropological studies have alerted the student of communities to the local distinctiveness of small rural settlements. For example, people's knowledge of each other is much more 'public' (Emmett 1964, 1982) in rural areas. The invading impersonalisation of urban people creates an alien obtrusive culture.

In location terms, the quality of rural life is characterised by intimate conventions, which establish idiomatic forms of proscription and prescription, especially in the less accessible and remote countrysides. Far from being idyllic, rural life in the less accessible and the remote countryside is often constraining and oppressive. A parochial rural tyranny can invade the most intimate and private circles. There may be parochialism in urban settings, but generally there is a higher social density where there is a lower density of population and 'vice versa'.

In the marginal areas of the less accessible and remote countrysides women are particularly isolated, either as in-migrant lone widows, whose retired husbands died relatively shortly after moving into the area, or they are younger mothers often without a car. Wife battering and incest cases may be no more frequent than in urban areas, but they are more difficult if not almost impossible to detect in the remote countryside. Giarchi (1990: 62-65) has demonstrated that 'distance decay' makes access significantly more difficult for either visits of clients to professionals or vice versa. In remote areas wives are certainly 'captive'. The traditional milieux are more constraining and patriarchy is more entrenched, particularly in pockets of 'feudal rural areas'.

The rural world has endemic peripheral social problems
The political rural landscape also has its own particular features. These were once more stable. De-population and re-population in rural areas create local political imbalances. Macro and micro politics alter when the countrysides alter. The point to stress is that both the de-population and re-population in rural areas are engineered from outside and usually from above. The remote and less accessible countrysides become accessible. As a result, the social boundaries of life are often in total disarray, as also are lives and local rural economies, to be dealt with in the next section of this chapter. Giarchi (1984) describes the machinations that shatter and alter the rural ways of life, when regionalisation dictated by centrist ideas shift boundaries. Cloke (1988) has commented upon the intervention of planners, bureaucrats and central government in rural areas.

Rural intervention is primarily carried out in favour of capital, property and class. Here rural policies are dictated by elitism, managerialism and structuralism. The management and planning are dictated by centrist policies to facilitate state control in local space. Structural controls dictated by the encumbant political party and Whitehall officialdom conserve the dominance of one class and their interests over others. Recent examples of such interventions are provided by various authors in *People in the Countryside*, edited by Champion and Watkins (1991). The political climate within the heartland counties of the South Midlands, East Anglia and South East England is essentially conservative. These counties were for the most part under Tory party control. In contrast, the rural localities at the margins, such as in Cornwall, Wales and Scotland, seek independence from centralised state control (from Thatcherism and Majorism) and are generally less favoured when priorities are decided upon in Whitehall. In the heartland rural areas, favouritism is enjoyed. It is in these, particularly, that the local elitist farming and landowning fraternities are being taken over by new Town Tories drawn from the vigourous entrepreneurial in-migrant service classes.

In addition to these outside centrist and elitist interventions, there are several long-standing peripheral problems. Walker (1978:6) on the basis of a rural development project in Hereford and Worcester listed six specific rural problems. He identified difficulties with:

(1) obtaining adequate water, particularly during droughts;
(2) purchasing food due to a lack of local shops, poor public transport and cutbacks in deliveries;
(3) buying or renting adequate housing of an acceptable standard at reasonable prices together with a shortage of council houses and more complex planning restrictions;
(4) meeting other people socially, due to the lack of meeting places, poor public transport and the lack of public telephones;
(5) obtaining suitable work, providing adequate income in an easily accessible location, exacerbated by restricted choices because of limited industries; and
(6) procuring adequate health/medical care due to centralised health services.

To these can be added five other rural problem areas on the basis of research carried out (The Association of County Councils, 1979; McLaughlin, 1983; Seed, 1984; Blacksell, Economides and Watkins, 1984; Watts, 1984; and Giarchi, 1987, 1990). They identify special rural difficulties in obtaining:

(1) personal social service care due to centralised specialisms in city and urban areas (Watts, 1984; Association of County Councils,

1979; Seed, 1984; ACORA, 1990);

(2) legal assistance and advice due to the centralised legal services in urban areas (Giarchi, 1988, 1990; Blacksell, Economides and Watkins, 1984);

(3) postal counter services due to the closure of many sub-post offices in rural areas (McLaughlin, 1983);

(4) opportunities to discuss benefits with social security officers, due to the concentration of DSS officers in urban areas (Giarchi, 1988, 1990);

(5) transport: in some counties as many as 24% of households do not have a car (Giarchi, 1988): the government's deregulation of the buses (1986) affects people's mobility; the elderly are faced with particular transport difficulties (Wenger, 1992).

In addition to the above general difficulties in rural areas, there is the major problem of 'lack of people'. For the elderly, this consists of a lack of volunteers and carers; for the young this consists of enough peers. These 'lacks' create difficulties across the rural counties of the UK, as reported by young people in an extensive survey in countrysides in twelve different counties: Cheshire, Cornwall, Gloucestershire, Hertfordshire, Leicestershire, Lincolnshire, Northamptonshire, Orkney, Ross-shire, Somerset, Suffolk, and Warwickshire (NAYC Campaign for Rural Youth, 1983). The lack of people also creates difficulties for rural older people, who as a result either have special socio-economic difficulties (Giarchi, 1989), whose health as a result is worse than in urban areas (Wenger, 1984 and Lassey & Lassey, 1988).

Although unemployment is a nationwide problem affecting urban and rural areas, there is evidence that unemployment hits the remote countryside most of all. Approximately 50% of young people are out of work in the rural areas of the French Alps, German Republic, Norway, Greece, Ireland and the UK (Eurosocial, 1985). Akehurst (1983) states,

> Taking Britain as a whole, rural unemployment levels are about 2% higher than urban unemployment levels.

The situation has worsened since the recession — peripheries suffer first.

Whatever the structural sociological explanations for discounting specific rural problems, there are socio-geographic and anthropological reasons for acknowledging the substantive difference between many urban and rural delivery problems. The rural problems call for corresponding qualitative differences in social service/health service provision and advice-giving arrangements in rural areas. However, as stated earlier the 'rural areas', as such, constitute four types of countryside. It is in these that the above factors establish varying degrees of rural deprivation and diverse needs for particular types of community work intervention.

Pacione (1984:201) has summed up the basic differences situationally in general terms:

> There are important differences in the nature of urban and rural deprivation, stemming mainly from basic contrasts in the physical and social environments. Thus, whereas the fundamental dimensions of urban deprivation are associated with problems of environmental decay, class and ethnic conflict, overcrowding, delinquency, criminality and social disorganisation, deprived rural areas suffer more from the problems of inaccessibility, social isolation, and the lack of a threshold population large enough to attract and maintain even the most basic village services and facilities.

The problems identified by Pacione clearly affect women in the less accessible and remote countryside, particularly mothers, more than men. If women are disproportionately deprived of their own means of transport in urban areas, they are doubly deprived of them in rural areas, where the repair of second cars is a crippling expense and usually consists of the 'wife's banger', which is often more unreliable and less comfortable than 'dad's' deluxe model.

Wenger (1984, 1992) has clearly demonstrated the enormous difficulties facing the elderly and carers in rural Wales. Her European studies now in process are demonstrating the same as those of Giarchi (1994). The transport problems in urban areas do not compare with those of the rural areas.

In anthropological terms, enough has been said to emphasise the social and cultural distance between the urban and rural cultures. Interestingly, Maclouf and Lion (1983) identified social and cultural distance as concomitants of geographic distance, on the basis not of grand theory, but of empirical studies in Wales, the West of Ireland and Southern France. More recent texts such as that of Cloke (1988) and Champion and Watkins (1991) have identified the same distance factor as a central feature.

However, the socio-economic construction of rural life must also be explored in comparative terms not only within a spatial context, but also within the context of power in local politics, where coalitions attract or oppose new capital penetrations (Pickvance 1983). These might also be identified and stratified by rural community workers within Russell's (1986) countrysides. The 'feudalism' of traditional rural areas protects 'beauty spots', creates

exclusive rights to a few rods on the rivers and permits only a select
few to enjoy the best environs. Injustices are rife in many rural areas.

Lastly, homelessness emerges as a recent rural phenomenon,
which at first sight appears to be anachronistic. Indeed, Lennon
(1991) has shown that homelessness in rural Cornwall is equal in
proportion to any within the inner cities. Rural housing has been
dramatically affected by a disproportionate decline in the availability
of rented rural accommodation; mortgage repossession in areas
where unemployment has been most severe; and 'the right to buy',
together with the cutback in the supply of council houses, have
seriously affected cheaper housing for poorer rural families and
single persons. Rural council housing is more seriously affected by
the privatisation of local county authority properties. As Lennon
(1991) points out, the private rented sector has failed to fill the gap.
Housing associations in 1989 only provided half as many dwellings
as they did in 1979. Referrals suggest that about 50% of all homeless
enquiries in rural Cornwall were mainly from such people as the
single homeless, couples with no dependents and/or people who
are sharing overcrowded, possibly substandard accommodation.
The local authority has no statutory duty to house these people,
unless their conditions are exceptionally severe. The homeless rural
are just one problem population whose presence is denied by both
the public and the administrators of welfare.

The rural world has need of specialised community workers
It has been necessary to discuss what is meant by 'rurality', and to
identify what is specific about 'rural deprivation'; it is also necessary
to examine whether there is a case for 'rural community action'.

The Bryants (1982: 45) in a pertinent paragraph described
community action as:

> a particular approach to organising local groups and welfare policies,
> an approach in which the political impotence or powerlessness of these
> groups is defined as a central problem and strategies employed which
> seek to mobilise them for the representation and promotion of their
> collective interests.

Community action is made possible in and through group processes.
CCETSW Paper 8 (1977) succinctly sums up the objective of
community action, stating that its aim is 'to make democracy work'
(para. 2.05). It also describes community action as 'group processes
occurring in the context of social welfare, which may take on an
explicitly political nature'. (para. 2.04). The purpose is to enable
groups in localities to make use of alternative means of securing
speedier, less expensive and more equitable services provided by

social security, housing and health care, 'to right the inequalities of power, wealth and knowledge'. (para. 2.06). The problem is that urban and rural areas are in competition for these resources. When economies are under consideration at times of 'cut-backs', peripheral areas suffer most. Rural interests are regarded as secondary to urban priorities. Urban budgets usually eclipse parish concerns. As a result, subsidised ventures in the urban shadow countryside suffer disproportionately, such as village child-minding schemes, volunteer drivers' rotas for rural vulnerable groups or families, rural day centres for older people, and drop-in venues for the unemployed. They are regarded as less significant to urban executives, on the basis of 'number-crunching' criteria, and not upon the degree of socio-economic need. This also may apply to constituencies, where urban needs outbid rural demands simply because MPs may feel the need to support the greater number of voters in the urban area rather than the lesser number in the rural surround.

There are four consequences resulting from a disregard of a distinctive rural particularism:
1) community work in rural settings is least resourced;
2) community work in rural settings is rarely researched;
3) community work in rural settings is seldom included as part of formulated policy;
4) community work in rural settings is not part of the training curriculum for the caring professions.

These consequences drove Ackhurst (1983) to complain that 'No one has written down a policy on rural youth'; that *rural* youth work as such is non-existent; and that 'there is no formal statement on the "rural youth problem" (1983: 32). With regard to the elderly, the *Report of the International Expert Group Meeting on Ageing in Remote Rural Areas* (Eymoutiers/Limoges, 1983) equally decried the lack of community strategies in the context of 'The specific nature of the difficulties of the elderly people in remote rural areas' (*Eurosocial Report* No.24, 1984). The case for specific policies and specialist training of workers in rural areas dealing with the young and the aged, was also made in an influential international expert group conference in Luz-Saint-Sauveur, France, March 1985 (Ribes, 1985).

The nature of rural community work
Attention has been paid so far in this discussion to:
1) the danger of throwing out the particularism of rural life with the urban-rural dichotomy;
2) the specific nature of rural deprivation; and

3) the need for a rural community work approach.

What are the implications of the above discussions in terms of carrying out community work/roles, tasks and skills in the four countrysides defined by Russell (1986)? It is commonly accepted in the major community work literature (e.g. Rothman and Jones, 1971; Henderson and Thomas, 1981; Bryant B, and R, 1982) that there are five community work roles:

1) enabler;

2) interpreter;

3) advocate;

4) negotiator;

5) planner.

The community worker has two main tasks:

1) *support local level organisation and innovation*

2) *to politically activate* (not agitate) *the local political forces in the locality.*

As a catalyst the community worker has nine main skills (Bryants 1982):

1) relational;

2) communication;

3) organisational;

4) mediating

5) bargaining;

6) entrepreneur;

7) research;

8) political;

9) tactical.

These are determined by the local way of life and by the customs and socio-economic settings. This is not the place to discuss the use of such roles and skills in any detail. Benfield (1990) and Francis and Henderson (1992) have provided an interesting commentary upon some of their usages.

Obviously, the ability to make meaningful contact is what matters. Roles and tasks establish the range of skills, but the weighting of these is determined by:

1) the ability to relate 'personal troubles to public issues' (Mills, 1959; Bryants, 1982);

2) the ability to relate 'personal troubles' to local issues.

The former is structurally oriented, and the latter is locationally oriented. Local issues in rural areas tend to be less confounded by the substantive urban issue. The latter are more directly linked with the infrastructural capitalist system (the city is the epitome of capitalism and is capitalism *par excellence* — Castells 1976).

There is one sector which ought to be cited as creating the greatest problems for the rural community worker: the need to mediate, negotiate and protest *from a position of strength*. The community worker in the urban setting is in a better position to call upon the support of the larger city/town political party. The larger urban electorate's concern over local problems is usually shared by larger numbers. Communities of interest are more easily galvanised in urban areas. In rural areas, particularly the less accessible and remote countryside, collective strength is often weaker. In situations where the worker is responsible for both urban and rural areas, there is also a great deal of pressure on the community worker to respond to urban problems which tend to overwhelm and take over the agenda. Lastly, there are two other factors worth considering.

There is a need at the macro level for the community worker to politicise rural issues to link with other workers and other voluntary agencies in other countrysides, and with people across the whole county and perhaps at times the whole country, so as to push rural issues out of village and church halls into the regional or national press and the Houses of Parliament, as was done to some extent by the one million alliance *Rural Voice* (1987). This is easier said than done, because of the low status of workers in rural areas (Dalton, 1987; Phillps and Williams, 1984) and the particular communication difficulties facing community workers in the less accessible and remote countrysides. Whereas farmers have been successful in exerting nationwide pressures upon policy makers, rural community workers have not been so successful. To galvanise a collective nationwide rural political front on behalf of employees in rural areas is more difficult to achieve because of the highly fragmented heterogeneous worker groups, the low-income profile and the disproportionate number of part-time employees (e.g. see Phillips and Williams, 1984: 20-21). Historically, there is also considerably less grass-roots rural support for more socialist supported worker movements. Knox (1982) has also shown how bureaucrats stifle the efforts of rural councillors. Community worker strategies must be established. Many rural areas are therefore considerably modified in areas where the roles of bureaucrats, councillors and worker groups contrast with those in the urbanised settings.

In addition to the above considerations, there is a need at the micro level to focus particularly upon the needs of women. The community work literature has not only an urban bias, but when it focuses upon rural settings it tends to be gender neutral. Sociological literature in rural areas which deal with womens' groups is scarce. Yet rural community workers know how vital rural womens' groups are. Women are very much out of sight as objects of oppression, especially in the less accessible and the remote countrysides. Research within this sector of concern is urgently required.

Amongst rural issues demanding attention, rural women have asserted their right to give birth to their babies at home. The Maternity Alliance in conjunction with the National Federation of Women's Institutes carried out a survey concerning this issue in 1989 as reported at the National Conference of the Maternity Alliance and the Women's Institute, Birmingham, Autumn 1989. Local maternity units have been closed down as maternity services are centralised. For the rural community worker this is surely a major issue. In addition, there is the need for community workers to facilitate the operation of the community care strategy. As stated earlier, the NCVO has complained that the 1990 Act did not consider the rural dimension. Who better than rural community workers to act as catalysts to bring about collaboration within the new plural welfare system within the four countrysides.

Conclusion
The case has been made for a *rural* community work approach to local problems in the countryside. Sociologists have presented arguments which indicate that there is no dichotomy between the urban and the rural (for example: Pickvance, 1978; Castells, 1976; Bulmer, 1986).

However, there are also qualitative differences between the social milieux of most countrysides and most urban settlements. Major social geographers (e.g. Pacione, 1984) and anthropologists (e.g. Cohen, 1982) have demonstrated that there are marked differences, especially because countrysides are more sensitive to the effects of distance decay. Rural deprivation and urban deprivation have much in common, but enough has been said to show that there are also social problems which are more salient in rural areas than they are in urban ones. In addition, the community care strategy and the peculiar problems affecting the rural areas, as discussed elsewhere by Giarchi (1990), call for community work involvement if the care of the elderly and the disabled in rural areas is to be both efficient and effective.

References
ACORA (Archbishops Commission on Rural Areas) (1990), *Faith in the Countryside*. Worthing: Churchman Publications Ltd.

Akehurst, M.D. (1983) *Groundwork.* National Association of Youth Clubs.

Association of County Councils (1979) *Rural Deprivation.* HMSO.

Bell, P. and Cloke, C.P. (1991), 'Public Transport in the countryside: the effects of bus deregulation in rural Wales', in T. Champion and C. Watkins, (eds) as below, pp.125;-143.

Benfield, G. (1990), *Rural Deprivation and Community Work* Occasional Paper, No.12, The School of Social Studies, University College, Swansea.

Berger, P. & Luckman, T. (1967) *The Social Construction of Reality.* Allen Lane.

Blacksell, M., Economides, K. & Watkins, C. (1984) 'Legal Services in Rural Britain: access, accessibility and need' *Working Paper, Access to Justice in Rural Britain,* Exeter University.

Bryant, R. & R. (1986) *Change and Conflict,* Aberdeen University Press.

Bulmer, M. (1986) *Neighbours,* Cambridge University Press.

Butler, J.E. & Fuguith, G.V. (1970) 'Small Town Population Change and Distance from Larger Towns, in *Rural Sociology,* 35, 396-409.

CCETSW Paper 8, (1977) *Social Work Curriculum Study,* Central Council for Education and Training in Social Work.

Castells, M. (1976) *The Urban Question,* Arnold.

Champion, T. and Watkins, C. (eds), (1991), *People in the Countryside, Studies of Social Change in Rural Britain.* Paul Chapman Pub. Ltd., London.

Cherry, G. (1976) *Rural Planning Problems.* Leonard Hill.

Clark, D.M. and Woollett, S. (1990), *English Village Services in the Eighties.* ACRE, Rural Development Commission, London.

Cloke, P.J. (1977) 'An Index of Rurality in England and Wales', *Regional Studies,* 11, 31-46.

Cloke, P.J. (1978) 'Changing Patterns of Urbanisation in the Rural Areas of England and Wales'. *Regional Studies* 2, 605-617.

Cloke, P.J. (1985), 'Whither Rural Studies?', *Journal of Rural Studies,* 1, 1-9.

Cloke, P.J. and Edwards G. (1986), 'Rurality in England and Wales 1981: A Replication of the 1981 Index, *Regional Studies,* (20), pp.289-306.

Cloke, P.J. (ed), (1988), *Policies and Plans for Rural people,* Unwin Hyman, London.

Cloke, P.J., Phillips and Rankin, D. (1991), 'Middle-class housing choice: channels of entry into Gower, South Wales', in T. Champion and C. Watkins (eds), as above, pp.38-52.

Cohen, A.P. (1968-1983) *Anthropological Studies of Rural Britain,* Economic and Social Research Council.

Cohen, A.P. (1978) 'Oil and the Cultural Account. Reflections on a Shetland Community', *Scottish Journal of Sociology,* Vol.3, No.1., pp.124-141.

Cohen, A.P. (1982) *Belonging,* Manchester: Manchester University Press.

Cullingford, D & Openshaw, S. (1982) 'Identifying Areas of Rural Deprivation Using Social Area Analysis'. *Regional Studies* 16(6).

Dalton, A.J. (1989) *Turn Left at Land's End.* Red Boots Publications.

Emmett, I. (1964) *A North Wales Village.* Routledge, Kegan and Paul.

Emmett, I. (1982) Chapters 7 and 8 in A.P. Cohen (ed) *Belonging,* Manchester University Press.

Eurosocial Report, (1984) No.24. European Centre for Social Welfare Training and Research.

Eurosocial Report, (1985) *Youth and Life in Remote Rural Areas,* Ribes Report No.27. European Centre for Social Welfare Training and Research.

Frances, D. & Henderson, P. (1992). *Working with Rural Communities,* Macmillan 1992.

Frankenberg, R. (1966) *Communities in Britain.* Penguin.

Freire, P. (1972) *Pedagogy of the Oppressed.* Penguin.

Friedland W. et al (1981) *Manufacturing Green Gold.* Cambridge University Press.

Gans, H.J. (1962) *The Urban Village.* New York Free Press.

Gant, R. and Smith, J. (1991), 'The elderly and disabled in rural areas: travel patterns in North Cotswolds', in T. Champion and C. Watkins, (eds), as above, pp 108-124.

Giarchi, G.G. (1984) *Between McAlpine and Polaris,* Routledge, Kegan and Paul.

Giarchi, G.G. (1986) 'The Effects of De-Industrialisation in Rural Areas' (unpublished paper, National Association of Citizen Advice Bureaux Conference, Nottingham University).

Giarchi, G.G. (1987), 'Cornwall's Gaza Strip: administrative and cultural constraints to geriatric care in a peripheral rural area', in S. di Gregorio, *Social Gerontology: New Directions,* Sage, London, pp.198-214.

Giarchi, G.G. (1988) *Information Deprivation in a Cornish Setting.* National Association of Citizen Advice Bureaux Study.

Giarchi, G.G. (1989) *Rural Deprivation in a Cornish Setting.* National Association of Citizen Adivce Bureaux Study.

Giarchi, G.G. (1990) 'Distance Decay and Information Deprivation: Health Implications for Rural People in Rural Isolation' in P. Abbot and G. Payne *New Directions in the Sociology of Health.* Falmer Press.

Giarchi, G.G. (1994) *Care of the Elderly in Europe.* Gower (forthcoming).

Grant, G. (1984) The Rural-Urban Dichotomy in Social Care. Rhetoric and Realisation, Lishman (ed). Social Work in Rural and Urban Areas, *Research Highlights No.9.* Aberdeen University Press.

Halmos, P. (1978) *The Personal and the Political.* Hutchinson.

Harper, S. (1986), 'The kinship network of the rural aged: a comparison of the indigenous elderly; and retired immigrant', Paper, British Society of Gerontology Conference, University of Glasgow, UK, 1986.

Harper, S. (1991), 'People moving to the countryside: case studies of decision-making', in T. Champion and C. Watkins (eds), as above, pp.22-37.

Hart, J.F. & Salisbury, N.E. (1965) 'Population Changes in Middle Western Villages and Statistical Approach' in *Annals of the Association of American Geographers* 55, 140-60.

Henderson, P. & Thomas, D.T. (1981) *Readings in Community Work.* London: George Allen and Unwin.

Homes, L. Review of A. Walker: in Rural Poverty, London: CPAS, *The Planner* 65: 82-3.

Joseph, A.E. & Phillips, D.R. (1984) *Accessibility and Utilisation.* Harper and Row.

Knox, P.L. (1982) *Urban Social Geography: An Introduction.* Longman.

Knox, P.L. & Cottam, B. (1981) 'Rural Deprivation in Scotland: a Preliminary Assessment'. *Tijdschrift voor Economische en Sociale Geografie* 72, 162-75.

Lassey, W.R. & Lassey, M.L. (1985) 'The Physical Health Status of the Rural Elderly' in Coward R.T. and Lee G.R. (eds): *The Elderly in Rural Society: Every Fourth Elder.* Springer Publishing Company.

Lennon, J. (1991), *The Homeless in Cornwall,* Cornwall Social Services Department, Truro.

Lennon, J. (1991), *Cornwall: Rural Deprivation,* Cornwall Social Services Department, Truro.

Lishman, J. (1984) *Social Work in Rural and Urban Areas.* Aberdeen University Press.

MacLouf P. & Lion, A. (1983) Ageing in Remote Rural Areas. A Challenge to Social and Medical Services. *Eurosocial Report,* No.24.

Massey, D. (1979) 'In What Sense A Regional Problem?', *Regional Studies,* 13, pp.233-244.

McLaughlin, B. (1983) *Country Crisis.* Media Services Unit: Natural Extension College.

Mill C. Wright, (1959). *The Sociological Imagination.* Oxford University Press.

NAYC and CRY (1983) *The Main Problem is Lack of People,* Nuneaton.

Newby, H. & Buttel, F. (1980) 'Toward a Critical Sociology' in Buttell and Newby (eds) *The Rural Sociology of the Advanced Societies. Critical Perspectives.* Croom Helm.

Ogburn, W.F. (1922) *Theories of Social Change.* B.W. Huebach.

Pacione, M. (1984) *Rural Geography.* Harper and Row.

Pahl, R.E. (1965) *Urbs in Rure.* Wiedenfeld and Nicholson.

Pahl, R.E. (1968) The Rural-Urban Continuum in R.E., Pahl (ed), *Readings in Urban Sociology.* Pergamon Press.

Pahl, R.E. (1966) The Rural-Urban Continuum in *Sociologica Ruralis,* Vol.6, N.3/4, pp.299-329.

Pickvance, C.G. (Ed) (1976) *Urban Sociology: Critical Essays.* Tavistock.

Pickvance, C. (1983) 'Spatial Policy as Territorial Politics', unpublished paper British Sociological Association Conference, University of Cardiff.

Redfield, R. (1944) *The Folk Culture of Yucatan.* Chicago University Press.

Redfield, R. (1955) *The Little Community: Viewpoints for the Study of a Human Whole.* Chigago University Press.

Redfield, R. (1960) *Peasant Society and Culture.* Chicago University Press.

Rees, G. (1984) Chapter 2 in *Locality and Rurality,* (eds Bradley T and Lowe, P). Geo Books.

Ribes, B. (1985) *Youth and Life in Remote Rural Areas: Eurosocial Report No.27.* European Centre for Social Welfare, Training and Research.

Rikkenen, K. (1968) 'Change in Village and Rural Population with Distance from Duluth' in *Economic Geography,* 44, 312-25.

Rothman, J. & Jones, W. (1971) *A New Look at Field Instruction,* Associated Press.

Rural Voice, (1987) *A Rural Strategy.* Fairford.

Russell, A. (1986) *The Country Parish.* SPCK.

Seed, P. (1984) Residential and Day Services: Change in a Changing Context in Lishman, J. (ed) *Research Highlights No.9,* Aberdeen University Press.

Shaw, J.M. (1979) *Rural Deprivation and Planning.* Geo Books.

Southall, A. (1959) 'An Operational Theory of Role' in *Human Relations,* Vol. XII No.1.

Stojanovic, S. (1973) *Between Ideals and Reality,* New York: (cited by P. Halmos: *The Personal and the Political.* Hutchinson 1978, No publisher given).

Tonnies, F. (1963) *Community and Society.* Harper and Row.

Walker, A. (ed) (1978) *Rural Poverty.* CPAG.

Watts, S. (1984) A Practice View in *Research Highlights No.9* (as above).

Wenger, C. (1984) *The Supportive Network: Coping with Old Age.* George Allen and Unwin.

Wenger, C. (1988) 'Support Networks in Old Age', in M. Jefferys: *Growing Old in the Twentieth Century,* pp.166-185. Routledge.

Wenger, C. (1992) *Help in Old Age: Facing up to Change.* Liverpool Univ. Press. Liverpool.

Worsley, P. (1987) *Introductory Sociology.* Penguin.

10

Community Organising in The United States

Coalescing a Diversity of Discourses

Ann Jeffries

As the 1980s drew to a close our attention was riveted to astounding scenes of people challenging authorities; people in communities across Eastern Europe coming out onto the streets, acting collectively with incredible courage to claim their democratic rights. One after another deeply entrenched authoritarian dictatorships crumbled. People acting locally were having a trans-national impact.

Subsequently we have been dismayed to see some of these same communities torn apart by the legacy of past passions, suppressed and unresolved, in deep freeze for all these years, suddenly resurfacing to complicate the horror of coping with the bankruptcy of the Soviet system. And, despite the initial thinly veiled gloating of Western leaders, the failure of Western democracies to address inequality and provide adequately for all its citizens also has been shockingly apparent in the turmoil of so many Western inner cities and in miscarriages of justice from Los Angeles to London.

Two aspects of such events form the threads drawing together this chapter. The first is the question of the way in which the vision and will for change is nurtured, especially amongst oppressed people. The second concerns the sustaining and renewal of democracy as well as the means necessary to ensure that action for change is owned by the people. How open are we in the West to discard old mind sets and solutions born in very different eras, in order to enable more equal people power in Western societies? What role does community work have in all this? Indeed, how adequate a guide is analysis based on the old alignments of industrialisation for community activists in the 1990s.[1] Finally, how does one hold the need for social and regional identity in creative tension with the need for concerted global action to bring about a more just and equitable society? These are crucial issues facing community work in the 1990s. Can developments in the US illuminate the debate in the UK?

Clearly in a world that is dominated by multinationals, with power bases that operate largely outside the democratic processes of any state, economic trends and environmental impacts show little respect for national boundaries. Developments in information technology have helped ensure that socio-political themes and fads flash rapidly from one country to another. Yet we remain remarkably blinkered when it comes to assessing the implications for and impact on community work. It seems incredible that more than twenty years after we first saw those stunning pictures of our 'space ship earth', we still lack a global perspective; a sense of our inter-dependence that far transcends national boundaries. It is this gap, in regard to trans-Atlantic understanding at least, that this chapter seeks to bridge. This is not to suggest that we should emulate the Thatcherite proclivity to import wholesale policies developed in and for different social and political cultures. Rather we need to risk moving beyond stereotypical views of the United States in order to really assess the relevance of developments there for community action on this side of the Atlantic.

The chapter first addresses a major stumbling block in this regard, namely the nature of the political and ideological context in which community work is undertaken in the United States. While activists in Britain have shown a tendency in the past to write off American community organising because of the apparent antipathy to socialism, is it possible that Americans actually may have been less shackled by ideological straight jackets or rigid mindsets and thus better poised to respond effectively in these times of rapid change? Or has pluralism resulted in ineffectual stalemate? With these questions in mind, a brief overview and analysis of the strengths and weaknesses of community organising trends in the USA will be followed by a more focused review of developments on three fronts: the civil rights movement; the women's movement; and with regard to homelessness. In the process it is intended that the empowering essence and transformative potential for community work will be elucidated.

The Context for Community Organising in the USA

> Our understanding of democracy has become dangerously narrow in this century. The liberal view of politics constructs society in terms of individuals and has defined democracy simply as the procedure whereby individual voters 'chose' their leaders. (Cawson; 1982 p.104)

This is a far cry both from the re-discovery of collective identities and grassroots action that swept Eastern Europe recently and from the concept of a liberal democracy that inspired American Independence. Then participative democracy, rather than representative democracy, was considered to be the key to a free society. A system of checks and balances was built into the structure of government as a guard against abuse of power by elected politicians as well as by administrators. Stress was placed on equality of opportunity. The continuing struggle in the USA has been about how to give that some semblance of reality in fact.

At the time of Independence there appears to have been a remarkably participative underpinning to the decision-making process.[2] Citizenship was not taken lightly. Ideally a citizen was someone who could take time out from personal concerns to focus on public affairs. Ironically, however, this principled attempt to guarantee government by the people also allowed elitism, particularly economic elitism, to develop: the right to property was justified as a means to ensure enough independence for citizens (albeit propertied white males) to participate in their self-governing communities. The government itself was viewed as the instrument of these community bodies which were the core of democracy.

The appearance of even this much political participation at the local level blinded people to the subtle centralisation of economic power. As the crushing response to early labour organising illustrated, when economic power was threatened the government supported the bosses. This split between a participative political process and centralised economic control has remained. Recognition of this dichotomy is crucial to an understanding of American politics and the social change process. As has been pointed out (Doern & Phidd 1983, Ch.2) core ideas and values that become entrenched in the psyche and structures of society may be eclipsed for a while but once embedded they tend to resurface in one form or another. Such core ideas will also play an important part in determining the fit of other ideas to that society.

A pertinent example was the failure of the United States to develop a socialist party. This has been a key difference and perhaps a major block to mutual understanding of community organising on each side of the Atlantic. The problem for Americans was not the stress on structural analysis. Although class analysis never seemed relevant enough to the experience of a majority of Americans to become widely accepted, the structural basis of poverty has been recognised consistently (eg. Cox & Garvin 1970, p.42 and Brager & Specht 1973, p.22). The disjuncture appears to have had more to do with the perceived prescriptions for action.

For many Americans large scale unions and political parties run by remote 'party machines' have never meshed easily with the ideology of participative community traditions. The 1992 Perot phenomenon is to the point here. In particular the Marxist stress on abstract solidarity and the suspicion that community ties and traditions were ideologically unsound in terms of the development of class consciousness, also seemed un-American to many (Evans and Boyte 1986, p.15 and 186). This may seem surprising in a country generally seen to be a rootless, melting pot. However, it does fit this early heritage of both a community focused, participative democracy and rugged individualism.

The 'melting pot' image is now considered by many to be more myth than reality. Freedom of religion ensured that immigrants nurtured their traditions and built powerful community networks of ethnic support. They also bought-in to the American dream of upward mobility. Many recent Oriental and some Hispanic immigrants have proved remarkably successful at it but, at the same time, their ethnic identification has continued. One consequence is that, as was all too clear in the Los Angeles riot of May 1992, cities and states are becoming further polarised with pockets of distinct racial and ethnic groups dominating particular areas. As was noted in *The Observer* article entitled Roots of a Riot (3 May '92) "no fewer than 76 languages are now spoken in Los Angeles schools". And the targets of black rage "were largely not the whites but the 300,000 Koreans in the city".[3]

These ethnic patterns have the effect of further complicating the picture politically. When combined with heightened gender and health cleavages, more differentiated work alignments, in addition to economic disparities and welfare based alliances, the possible collective identities around which to organise become quite daunting. As Hall and Jacques note:

> the very proliferation of new sites of social antagonism makes the prospect of constructing a unified counter-hegemonic force as the agency of progressive change, if anything, harder rather than easier. (Hall and Jacques, 1989, p.17)

It is just this sort of complexity that gave rise to issue based politics in the States. "Issue Publics", to use the phrase coined by Philip Convers back in 1964, fit well with the participative tradition:

> . . . citizens define their own issue agenda. The issues might be as broad as nuclear disarmament or as narrow as the policies of the local school district. Citizens not elites decide. In short the communal mode shifts control of participation to the public and thereby increases citizen influence in the political process. (Dalton, 1988, p.45)

In a culture where political parties have never been such cohesive units as they have in Britain, issue publics became an important aspect of citizen politics. Shifting political alignments could be accommodated and there was more flexibility to allow for realistic commitments of time and energy. Citizens were seen to be 'satisfying' their political needs, balancing the costs and benefits of participation, by focusing on their own political interests. This is particularly appealing in America where "the heterogeneity of American parties lessens the policy value of party voting" (Dalton, 1988, p.29). With issue politics, people can build their own group, with its own membership, outside party structures.

Thus, while this sort of political organising could be said to be an expression of the general disillusionment with both the major parties and their leaders — as was so stunningly illustrated in the appeal of Ross Perot — it does mesh with the sense that the political and socio-economic environment is so complex and dynamic that a long term, comprehensive strategy is unrealistic. While such conclusions have been problematic from a traditional socialist perspective, they fit with the evolutionary theories of the natural sciences, the experience of feminists and with recent developments in business management. Here the stress is on the value of diverse viewpoints and the need for flexibility, adaptability and the ability to 'thrive on chaos'. While the business focus is on the importance of trial and error, feminists have come to see diverse analytical perspectives as more enriching than increasing the relevance of feminist analysis and, so long as this is coupled with a commitment to collaborate, broadening its action base.

This suggests that intense intellectual battles as to the best ideological engine to generate the 'New Society' are beside the point — a sentiment with which post modernists would concur. The potential sites for action and the bases of identification are both too particular and too profuse to fit into any ideological box. The dream of revolution which seemed so tantalisingly possible in the late 1960s is not so much an impossible dream as an inappropriate dream. Perhaps this is the explanation for the much criticised failure of the Left to develop "a popular, modernising perspective to coalesce disenchantment with the post-war settlement" (*New Times*, p.31). This failure to understand how much times have changed has meant that many Socialist intellectuals have been mesmerised by analysis to the point of despair and, by denigrating other change-oriented approaches, have precluded the possibility of the gradual transformation of society.

While Eastern Europe has provided dramatic evidence of the powerful potential of relentlessly "pushing against the bulwarks" of the establishment,[4] it has also shown the limitations of change without transformation. Likewise the Los Angeles riots of 1992 illustrate the paucity in a pluralistic, capitalist society of the reform approach as espoused, for example, by Brazier and Specht (1973, p.61). In these circumstances reform efforts so easily become a matter of push and shove as one group's successful tactics are superseded by those of another. If the economic/status odds are stacked, the outcome should not be surprising. For example the awakening of Middle America to community organising and issue politics was largely occasioned by negative backlash to the wide array of anti-poverty programmes which had been rushed in as part of President Johnson's Great Society plans, in the wake of inner-city rage at the snail-like pace of change in their situation. Hopes and expectations had been raised by the Black Civil Rights Movement but for people in the inner cities little changed. They exploded. The government responded. Middle America reacted.

This backlash reflected traditional American ambivalence about the role of government as well as deep seated racial attitudes. Elected leaders were seen to be too far ahead of the people. In such a pluralistic society it is hardly a coincidence then that at the same time as the War on Poverty went into retreat:

> organisation among middle Americans, particularly among ethnic sub-groups, has emerged as an area of current, direct, local community organising activity. (Grossner, 1976, p.244)

Thus the seventies ushered in the 'consumer' movement in the States. Ralph Nader spearheaded the action, initially taking on automobile manufacturers. It struck a chord with middle class consumers across the country and received tremendous support from people frustrated at their powerlessness with massive corporations and big government. The lessons of this expert-led action, combined with experience and insights drawn from the organisational efforts on the anti-Vietnam peace front, from Saul Alinski, from women and Black Americans, provided the impetus both for other disenfranchised groups to organise (such as Mexican farmworkers, the elderly, gays and disabled people) and for a new wave of neighbourhood based community development efforts (often in the form of Community Development Corporations), as well as more militant social action organising.[5]

Key ingredients in their organising strategies were a grounding in the expressed concerns and values of people banding together in groups that were separate from normal, political and bureaucratic channels. By also forming links with like-minded groups across the country they were better poised to influence public opinion, policy and funding. While the Women's Movement in particular has led the way in linking grassroots activity to sophisticated, strategic networking and political action at both state and federal level, various "issue publics" have been linking up to develop a broader agenda around which they can coalesce, maximising lobbying effect. Powerful examples are the 'stand up and take charge' movement in Texas, the 'Grey Panthers' (the senior citizens' lobby and watchdog organisation), the Industrial Areas Foundation (see Boyte, 1989) and the 'Independent Living Movement'. The latter is comprised of groups of people with various disabilities who had come together to support each other locally and campaign nationally in order to make normalisation more of a reality.

Neighbourhood work too in the eighties, though locally rooted, took a broader co-ordinated, strategic stance. Across the political spectrum in the United States people apparently appreciated the importance of community development and organisational skills. For example, in the 1970s and 1980s Saul Alinski's organisation of Industrial Areas Foundation (IAF) began to focus their efforts on "the moderates" in their existing institutions (largely their churches), in recognition of the importance of such vital mediating institutions for sustained community development and empowerment (see also Boyte, 1989, p.93). It is to the point in this regard that not only did 90% of social work students at the University of Michigan choose community organisation as their minor area of specialisation in the 1980s but this traditionally left-orientated faculty saw an influx of right-wing students.[6] Upon graduation they were quickly hired by a variety of right-orientated community based organisations.

Similarly, of course, in the United Kingdom, the New Right co-opted much of the language traditionally associated with more left-orientated community work — 'community' became the fashionable prefix; empowerment, participation and consumer choice are now right-wing terms. In other words the Right has seen the potential of these proven organising skills and concepts for forwarding their own agenda. Thus it is hardly surprising that after all this community based activity in the United States in the 1980s, the gap between the rich and poor (very poor whites as well as blacks) has grown. Indeed as an article by Prof. Patterson (Harvard University) and Prof. Winship (Northwestern) in the *New York Times* 3 May, 1992, entitled "White Poor, Black Poor" noted:

> The symptoms of moral and social chaos increasingly apply to the less visible, predominantly rural and suburban white underclass . . . By dividing the poor along racial lines and making poverty a black problem, we obscure the growing chasm between rich and poor in this country

. . . and reinforce the myth that poverty is a moral problem that only the poor themselves can solve.

However, before we give up on community organising let us not forget that while the Right might be using the language there are crucial differences in their understanding of the dynamic. In Neo-Conservative terms the community is static, the bastion of middle class morality and values. The involvement of the 'active citizen' is carefully prescribed. It applies to certain types of citizens who can be counted on to adopt good capitalist behaviour and take responsibility for their immediate family members. This sort of active citizen is needed to counteract the 'tyranny of the collective'. Their success serves to justify tougher controls on those who, 'failing' to make it in the system, lash out in anti-social ways. (Joy riders are an example of this in the UK). The claims of the underclass then can be ignored.

It is to the point that Reagan encouraged consumer action rather than citizen activity in the political sense (Boyte, 1989, p.79). The emphasis was on self-sufficiency and community responsibility within the context of the market place. This is a far cry from empowering community development which stresses mutual support and awareness-raising as a precursor for participation by diverse, free thinking citizens coalescing strategically to bring about tangible local social and economic development. This would be fostered by a government that endeavours to be the instrument of all the people. Here community life would be recognised as dynamic, complex and fluid, full of diversity, contradictions and pitfalls for the community organiser, but also the potential source for transformative social change. People would be empowered in relation to the institutions and agencies that impinge on them in their daily lives; in regard to their economic circumstances; and crucially, in their self-esteem. With this in mind a closer examination of the key elements in community organising in the USA ·is necessary. Is this sort of empowerment and community development apparent? If so, how is it fostered and maintained?

Organising in Specific Contexts: the Sources of Empowerment
Sara Evans and Harry Boyte (1986) in their book *Free Spaces: the sources of democratic change in America* contend that Americans have drawn repeatedly upon 'the great wells of democracy that were dug deep by the founding fathers' (Martin Luther King in King, C.S. 1984). The location of those wells, they suggest, is the community meeting places, (like the Independent Living Resource Centres set up by disabled people and the Black Churches in the

southern states). These provide a space which give freedom from the dominant culture, where people can come together, participate in their own way, share concerns, hopes and courage, foster self-esteem and a communal vision, develop and practice skills and, when the time is ripe, take action and forge wider links that can result in the transformation of their society. In Antonio Gramsci's terms, in these spaces people develop and can articulate a discourse that is theirs and which becomes the empowering essence of their action for social change. In Industrial Areas Foundation (IAF) organising this link between vision and power is acknowledged to be crucial. Their organising tactics take local traditions and religious values as the starting point for action and reflection in a strategic education process. For many in Eastern Europe too it appears that the Church helped keep alive such alternative visions.

Amongst African Americans an awareness of the importance of a vision for oppressed people was evidenced by the Black churches and others such as Marcus Garvey long before Martin Luther King's time. In the fifties and sixties the Nation of Islam or Black Muslims/Black Panthers, led by Malcolm X with his unabashed espousal of violence if necessary, as well as Black pride, were a potent prod to the white power structure to work with more moderate Black Christian leaders.

To effectively foster such a change process, even in a democracy, calls for an astounding range of competencies. As Jennifer Sayer (1986) points out, the challenge for community workers, whose jobs are at the interface between the institutional and the informal, is to enable people to make the crucial connections. This involves practically making the key organisational links and enabling people to make connections in terms of their awareness — in Freire's terms (1972), to develop a critical consciousness, to explore and recreate their own vision and a realistic strategic plan that leads towards its achievement. As Gramsci knew:

> for change to occur (either in the nature of hegemony, or in 'cementing' ideology) then work has to be done on both institutional practices, and on informal practices in civil society. (Sayer, 1986, p.296)

While the experience of Black Americans points to the importance of a place, free from interference, where people could nurture and articulate their own ideology, it is of course feminists who have stressed the importance of process and starting from personal experience as the precursor to critical awareness and the motivation for collective action. IAF organisers also constructively foster both anger and self-interest as spurs for collective action (Boyte, 1989). Feminists on both sides of the Atlantic place great importance on the process through which consciousness-raising and community development occurs. How we work is every bit as important as what we work on:

> . . . socialist feminists consider organising to raise consciousness and coalition building is insufficient without organising each group to meet their physical and species needs in ways that are alternative to existing systems of domination. (Nes and Iadicola, 1989, p.15)

It is also clear as one considers the history of feminist, black and populist movements in the States that this consciousness raising, community building, ideology articulating work may be all that happens for a very long time. Paulo Freire stresses that much work is needed before people realise that they are "in a situation". As he puts it:

> only as this situation ceases to present itself as a dense, enveloping reality . . . can people come to perceive it as an objective, problematic situation — only then can commitment exist. (Freire, 1972, p.81)

It also takes time for people to appreciate the potential for change that praxis posits and to discover appropriate action. Nor is it merely a matter of building sufficient momentum for people to risk taking action, it is also a matter of timing and developing skills in sensing and taking advantage of windows of opportunity for change. Outcomes in China and Eastern Bloc countries in 1989 provided tragic, dramatic examples of the difference getting this sort of assessment right can make. It is to the point that the Black churches in the southern states had nurtured a culture of resistance for hundreds of years before Rosa Parks sat down on that bus in Montgomery, providing the spark that ignited the Civil Rights Movement. Other attempts had been made over the years. The frustration of African Americans, returning from the Second World War to the same segregated society, added momentum. Black Americans had proved themselves on the battlefield and in the factories but still things had not changed yet. It was 1955 before all the threads came together and the timing was right for action to escalate, finally arousing, thanks largely to TV, the conscience of white America.

The Civil Rights Movement Revisited — how did they do it?

In the long-term, what did they achieve? Much has been made of Martin Luther King's adaptation of Mahatma Gandhi's practice of non-violent action and resistance and King's application of Alinksy-style creative targeting of actions; not so widely known was the painstaking behind-the-scenes work to hone the skills and attitudes necessary for success. Songs as well as speeches that stressed the way their challenge was based in biblical and American values, kept morale high and vision clear. Protesters were prepared for their violent treatment and schooled in non-violent response by role plays before every demonstration. Central to the movement were citizenship schools that taught literacy through the study of the Declaration of Independence. By its relevance to their cause the subject matter simultaneously enhanced motivation to learn and validated their aspirations. In the process of learning the skills necessary to register and vote, these people nurtured a vision of what could be. As a result they became self-conscious and self-confident: they empowered themselves.

It may have taken far too long to get to that point, but when the door was finally pushed ajar, the people were ready. The extent of activity from a people labouring under segregation was remarkable. For example by the summer of 1963, in the aftermath of the massive demonstrations and arrests in Birmingham, Alabama . . . non-violent direct-action campaigns had occurred in over 900 cities and towns, with an estimated one million participants. (Evans and Boyte, 1986, p.66)

That doesn't just happen. It takes committed, persistent, simultaneous and widely dispersed effort at the grassroots. This is the precursor to coalescence and it is the particular contribution that community work can make. It is the well spring of democratic change.

In recent years it has become commonplace to suggest that little has changed in America for Black people (eg. Pinkney, 1984). In fact many African Americans did take advantage of the removal of barriers to upward mobility. Substantial changes occurred in the law regarding educational and employment equity and have been consolidated. Crucial enforcement procedures were built in and well resourced, as is evidenced by the 'strong, affluent black middle class' (*The Guardian*, 24 July 1989). However, as the Rodney King beating illustrates, constant vigilance is required at all levels of society. Too many whites became complacent or resentful. Too many never changed.

Generally too in the seventies in the USA the focus was on heightening personal awareness — and this included a focus on one's own particular group's experience of oppression. Thus "identity politics" obscured the vision of an integrated society and blatant racism increasingly reared its ugly head again in the eighties. For example many universities had to renew their struggle with overt as well as institutional racism and review affirmative action programmes in order to come closer to reflecting minority population figures in their academic staff and student enrolment.

Neither can one overlook the effect of the economic down-turn and significant changes in urban aid. The tide really turned when President Carter's $30 billion 3-year plan was rejected by Congress in 1977. Over the Reagan years, direct aid to cities by the Federal Government was cut by some 60%. Whereas the Kerner Commission reporting after the riots of 1967, stressed that the cause of the problem was white racism and warned that the United States could become "two societies, one black, one white — separate but unequal" the consensus is that the situation revealed by the 1992 Los Angeles riot is much more complex. While the situation within the ghetto is even worse now than in the 1960s, the underclass constitutes a smaller proportion of the black population. The facts are that power relationships were shifted by the Civil Rights Movement. One must remember that the goals at that time were basic civil rights. In this there was considerable success. But what was also clear was the limitations of this movement. Significantly Martin Luther King was assassinated as he tried to broaden the base of activity to include issues of economic power. It was back to the bases, but certainly not back to square one for African Americans. Massive registration of black voters was achieved. Individually and through class action, educational and employment rights were extended. The employment of minority people and women increased much more dramatically in workplaces that came under federal anti-discrimination regulations than in ones that did not (Grant, 1988, pp.55-8). Not least of all the claim that "Black is Beautiful" was internalised. In short, the gains made have meant that Black Americans are visibly active at all levels of society and in all professions in the United States (Farley, (1984), p.194). Nevertheless even African Americans with college degrees earn only $798 for every $1000 earned by whites with similar qualifications. (*Guardian Weekly* 10.5.92)

However it is clear that the Civil Rights Movement went beyond merely helping individuals "to adjust to society", as is claimed by some.[7] Several of the largest cities have long been run by black administrations, for example Coleman Young in Detroit, Rice in Seattle, David Dinken in New York and of course Mayor Bradley in Los Angeles. Virginia has a black governor, Douglas Wilder, and Jesse Jackson mounted a serious bid for President in 1988 which would have been unthinkable in 1968. In the primaries he won the predominantly white states of Nevada, Vermont and Alaska. It is disillusioning, however, to see that in 1992 the Democrats concluded that they needed neither a Black American nor a woman on their Presidential ticket. The Democrats obviously consider attractiveness to white middle America is still the key to success (*Guardian Weekly* 1.5.90).

Furthermore, 31.3 per cent of black Americans still fall below the poverty line, compared to 11.4 per cent of white Americans and 29 per cent of Hispanics (Census, 1986b). 45% of black children but only 16% of white children live below the poverty line, even though the median income of a black family has gone up 5 per cent compared to a rise of 1.7 per cent for white families. However this was still an average income of only $16,790 compared to $19,030 for the average Hispanic family and some $29,150 for whites (Census, 1986a). Why?

Part of the problem is the hollowness of the victory achieved by electing African Americans to administrative responsibilities for cities which then had to cope with the massive cutbacks in urban aid and rising unemployment. African Americans trapped in the inner city 'under-class' are worse off than ever (Pinkey 1987, p.115). This is an even more complex problem now, compounded by, or reflected in, the 'crack' phenomenon. While there is a large variation between cities as to the extent crack could be said to be a problem,[8] the departure of upwardly mobile Black Americans from the ghettos — the success stories of the Civil Rights Movement — meant that the black role models, for achieving success by applying oneself within the system, were removed. Add to this the tension of the influx of people with other ethnic origins; combine this with the shocking unemployment figures in inner city areas and the appeal of the drug scene is understandable. Among black teenagers in the core South Central area of Los Angeles the unemployment rate was 43.8% in 1990, compared to 5.8% in Los Angeles County. It is a vicious circle. Inner city youth gangs find ways to get money and this enhances their 'street cred' and leads to the obvious conclusions that education is pointless, a 'whitey thing'.

Resentment at the comparative success of Oriental immigrants certainly fuels inner city tensions. Newcomers with close family networks tend to apply themselves with great diligence to making the American dream a reality, taking over neighbour corner shops in the only areas they can afford initially: the ghettos. Because of their loyalty to their extended families they do not need to employ other locals. It is to the point that a Korean shopkeeper in Los Angeles who had shot and killed a black youth, also received what was popularly perceived to be a light sentence not long before the Simi Valley verdict. Hence, when the Rodney King verdict was delivered feelings in the area were already raw.

Thus in various ways 'race continues to be an ever-present part of the American way of life' (Pinkney 1987, p.x). However, there are some encouraging signs too. For example, initial polls following the 1992 Los Angeles riots suggested that there was more similarity than difference in the reaction of blacks and whites to the beating and acquittal of the police, certainly a lot more similarity than African Americans expected. Nevertheless, there is clearly a long way to go simply to keep Martin Luther King's dream alive, let alone realise it for all African Americans. As the politicians finally seem to be recognising, dramatic action is needed for the ghettos. Action taken by the founder and formerly Chief Executive for forty years of The Rouse Company, typifies the sort of privately led response that would be widely supported by conservative governments both sides of the Atlantic.

Following the example of women tenants of public housing in Washington, D.C. who pioneered the much heralded Jubilee Housing development, Jim and Patty Rouse formed the Enterprise Foundation in 1982 to bring together private finance and neighbourhood groups in projects across the USA to "provide fit and affordable housing for the very poor". As their 1991 Annual Report indicates, after 10 years, over 17,250 decent, affordable homes are on their way to being rehabilitated or built new by non-profit groups in the network. More than 900 individuals, foundations and corporations have provided over $429 million to finance housing for low-income people.

Interestingly, the Enterprise Foundation sees housing as the starting point but recognises that this must go hand in hand with other community opportunities and services. So they have a Community Services Department and a Public Policy Department which works to bring in supportive legislation such as the National Affordable Housing Act (1990) and to extend Low-Income Housing Tax Credit. The fundamental theme is to challenge the pervasive pessimism about the ghettos, namely that "these conditions are uncorrectable — too complex, too costly."

Women Organising in the USA
It is a daunting task to try to keep up with the extent and variety of organisations and activity among women in the 1990s. The pattern of active local groups with national co-ordinating offices is a long established practice for organisations such as the American Association of University Women (1886), the Business and Professional Women (1919) and the League of Women Voters (1920). A key development in the eighties was the increased efforts to forge networks and formal coalition across the socio-economic,

ethnic and ideological spectrum. This represents an important breakthrough. There was a period when the stress on the 'personal is political' had the unfortunate consequence (in terms of strategic organising) of increasing fragmentation among women activists. As it became clear that earlier efforts had marginalised many groups of women the focus switched to the articulation of different experiences of oppression and the integrating vision was lost for sometime.[9] However as the eighties drew to a close, re-invigorated connections were being made, hand in hand with an appreciation of the richness in diversity. The importance of this refusal to be locked into a rigid ideology should not be minimised. To my mind it is a key contribution to the way forward.

Women networking in the USA now ranges from a variety of women's groups in one city sharing a building and newsletter, to a National Association of Women's Centres, (connecting multi-racial, multi-ethnic centres in 41 states) or the Women's Action Alliance (which gives support and technical assistance and facilitates an information exchange for women's organisations across the country).[10]

The North American Family Resource Coalition (1983) based in Chicago played a similar role for neighbourhood-based programmes for women with young children. These "drop-in" centres for parents and their children seemed to spring up in various guises across the continent in the Seventies. The key ingredient was again a place, preferably in the immediate neighbourhood, for parents with their young children to drop-in. Whilst ostensibly focusing on enriching opportunities for children, the centres (often a community house on a public housing estate) also gave women a space and a chance to reflect together on their situation. What Freire calls 'conscientisation' could begin. The Family Resource Coalition, with its focus on political pressure on behalf of families, was an outcome: grassroots groups linking up in partnership with professionals, to develop high-powered, political strategies.

The experience of black women in the US was in many crucial respects different to that of white women. Not only did racism overshadow everything but young black girls traditionally were encouraged to be independent. This was in part an historical consequence of slavery. As Angela Davis points out:

> there was no gender-based division of labour during slavery. And in the aftermath of slavery, proportionately far more black women worked for a living than white women . . . Black women activists did not have to learn to be assertive. (Davies 1989, p.70)

Black women felt little connection to the white women's need to overcome the gender-based sense of inferiority. Indeed black women were actually blamed for playing a domineering role in the "Negro Family" (Daniel Moynihan report, 1963). Furthermore key white feminist issues, such as rape, actually had the questionable consequence for black women of increased police presence in neighbourhoods conditioned to experiencing the police as enemies.

Nevertheless sexism was enough of a problem in the Black Power Movement to bring about the death of the Student Non-violent Co-ordinating Committee (SNCC) Los Angeles chapter (Davis 1989, p.68). Some women created their own organisations such as the Black Women's Alliance (later known as the Third World Women's Alliance) which focused on racism, sexism and imperialism (Davis, p.69). Today increasing numbers of women of colour are joining a more collaborated women's movement.

Black women tenants in many large cities who, in desperation at the abysmal state of public housing estates, skilfully took over management of their estates, have also developed grassroots based networks around the country. Their aim is to promote better housing for poor and low-income women and to enhance women's understanding of ways to improve their communities. Impressive community economic development projects as well as tenant management schemes have resulted (for details see Feit, Ronnie and Patterson 1985, p.185; and Checkoway 1985, p.225-256). To this end, for example, a neighbourhood based college programme was set up in New York in 1977 particularly for women tenants. Hundreds of women have completed this programme.

The organisation that was probably regarded as the standard bearer for the white Women's Movement was NOW — the National Organisation for Women started in 1966 in Washington, D.C, by a small group of women that included Betty Friedan. It mushroomed as other women's consciousness-raising, support groups, study groups and reproductive rights groups formed NOW chapters in communities across the country.

With the passage of the Equal Rights Amendment (ERA) by the Senate in 1972, the focus for NOW became the ratification of ERA by at least 38 states. By the 1982 deadline only 35 states had ratified and ERA could not be added as an amendment to the Constitution. This failure is indicative both of the deep-seated ambivalence regarding the status of women[11] and of the difficulties inherent in 'acting globally' on behalf of such a huge and diverse constituency. The ERA failure also illustrates the importance of timing. ERA coincided with the increasing fragmentation of the Women's Movement. For black women and women of colour, as well as working class and lesbian women, there were major flaws in the analysis and actions of dominant feminists. "Sisterhood" was problematic and NOW membership declined. Nevertheless large numbers of women could still be mobilised, for example in support of women's 'Right to Choose'. NOW has been at the forefront of state legislative abortion battles brought on by the very well organised anti-abortion lobby.

Some NOW city chapters, in addition to their work on the political front, set up separate branches or separate funds for non-political service work in areas such as women's health or comprehensive job training programmes and advocacy. Foremost among these is the NOW Legal Defense and Education Fund (LDEF) set up in 1970. LDEF aims to make the legal system less oppressive to women. As a result

> in 1984, nearly every law school in the US offered speciality courses in gender discrimination, and judicial training courses on sex bias have reached judges in every state. (Jane Grant 1988, p.71)

Through its Project on Equal Education Rights, LDEF also serves in a watchdog capacity regarding education for girls. NOW is not alone in stressing the importance of legal action in support of women's rights. There are numerous other legal advice centres and law projects across the county, such as the Women's Legal Defense Fund (Grant, 1988, *ibid*).

Throughout the seventies and eighties many women also invested considerable time and energy in the environmental and peace causes. Even such a cursory overview of women organising in the USA, must mention in particular the impressive work of groups such as WAND (Women's Action for Nuclear Disarmament). Again the focus was local support groups, local education projects, local and state demonstrations for peace and justice as the foundation for high profile, political pressure at the federal level. What is encouraging for the 1990s is the clear recognition that these are all aspects of the larger struggle for social change (Davis, 1989; Adams, 1989).

Wider Opportunities for Women (WOW) (1964), is another influential organisation. Despite an initial focus on college-educated women who wanted to return to part-time work, WOW took on board the criticism and changed its orientation to low-income and minority women. A key strategy is to encourage unskilled women to take up training in areas not normally employing women — for in these sectors pay will be better. Other tactics to facilitate women's home and employment needs have been job sharing and V-time (voluntary reduced work time for specified periods of time). Fair pay, focusing on specifying comparable job worth, will continue to be a focus for activity in the 1990s.

A relative newcomer to the scene (1980) is the Older Women's League (OWL). In addition to mutual support locally, OWL has a political agenda which reflects six key areas identified as current priorities by women in local chapters.

As indicated earlier, political agenda building has been a widespread development in the 1980s. Another example is the Women's Economic Agenda Project (WEAP) started in California in 1983. The strategy involved grassroots groups defining their economic issues and needs. This economic agenda was publicly debated by all representatives of WEAP before a pooled version is adopted. Local education and development followed — leading to extensive grassroots organising.

Membership of WEAP is welcome to organisations as long as they can support eighty per cent of the final agenda. By 1985 eighty organisations were involved. California WEAP had the satisfaction of seeing seventeen bills pass at the state level. By stressing economic matters, the agenda appears to be a successful strategy for developing a measure of unity. The goal of economic dignity for women apparently can become the basis for a common vision. The approach is being tried in other states too, for example, North Carolina.

The other area in which feminists have blazed an impressive trail is in opening up private funding sources for women's organisations. This involved work with major foundations and trusts as well as a protracted struggle to gain entry into the lucrative world of payroll giving. In the United States employees can reduce their taxable income by making a donation to a charity. For over a hundred years the "United Way" was the voluntary organisation that was the conduit for such funds. Working through a network of local branches with massive annual fund-raising campaigns run in each town by local volunteers, impressive amounts of money were committed each year. Employees could be under considerable pressure to make a pledge and, as the United Way tended to be conservative, a consequence was that it was harder for progressive groups and causes to get funds. In an effort to open up a way for working women to have their charitable giving go to help other women, Women's Way was launched in 1977. United Way eventually compromised allowing contributors to specify where their donation should go. By 1986 Women's Way was getting some one million dollars from payroll giving annually. Nevertheless it was estimated that by 1986 still "only four per cent of the billions of dollars donated by foundations in the US goes to the benefit of this group (women and girls)" (Grant, p.27). One wonders then how much of this reaches poor women in the rural and urban underclass.

This naturally raises questions as to the degree to which women's organisations have fallen prey to the trap of institutionalisation and their action for change contained in the very act of inducing big business to make resources available for women's programmes. It is unclear to what degree funding imperatives have become the means to assimilate women's organisations into bureaucratic (male) business management procedures, turning feminist activists into administrators and curtailing action for fundamental change. These questions have crucial implications in terms of the development of effective Social Movements and call for constant political clarity and vigilance (See Ng, Walker and Muller, 1990).

It is essential to hold all this within the context of increasing poverty. The 1970s not only signalled the abysmal failure of the War on Poverty, but actually sowed the seeds for tremendous growth in poverty in the United States. This was compounded by the policies of the Reagan and Bush administrations. For the purposes of this chapter, housing provides a pertinent illustration of the extent of the problem and an example of community organising efforts under the safety net.

Organising under the Safety Net with the Homeless

Nixon reintroduced doubts about the federal role in housing provision. Reagan completed the task. For a country which already put very little into the stock of public housing, the direction Reagan pursued seems nothing short of tragic.[12] There is a crying need for more low-income housing units. Demand for subsidised units far exceeds supply (Burghardt and Fabricant, (1987), p.24-5). Visitors to most large cities in the United States have long been confronted by dramatic visual evidence that the free enterprise system does not naturally respond to this demand. Indeed one has come to associate American cities as much with homeless people crouched over heating vents on the sidewalks, poking into garbage cans, taking over the subway stations, as one did twenty-five years ago with skyscrapers and flashy automobiles. To make matters worse, the homeless now are not just alcoholics or drug-users. They have been joined in increasing numbers by single parent families whose public assistance money does not keep pace with rising rents; with young and middle-aged unemployed men; with psychiatrically disabled people left homeless as institutions closed in the 1970s. The most dramatic increase in homelessness during the 1980s however was among those who fitted into the Aid for Dependent

Children (AFDC) category. "AFDC payments are between twenty per cent to sixty per cent below prevailing urban rents" (Burghardt 1987, p.25). Cities reported dramatic increases in eviction rates over this period. In New York fifty per cent of these proceedings involved families receiving public assistance and the number of homeless families rose from less than 500 to 3,200 in six years.

The most prevalent response to increasing homelessness has been the provision of emergency shelters and soup kitchens — visions of the 1930s. Such efforts have often been spearheaded by church and voluntary bodies which is precisely what Reagan wanted. However, as was starkly evident in the 1930s, churches and charities do not have the resources to meet more than a tiny fraction of the need. Response by all three levels of government has been woefully inadequate and a gaping chasm exists between supply and demand let alone need. (Borgos 1986, p.433).

Community workers try to move beyond provision of crisis assistance to focus on the basic need for permanent housing and income. Advocacy and coalition building are key strategies. An advocacy organisation, the National Coalition to House the Homeless, was formed to focus activity on the legal front. The Enterprise Foundation's efforts (mentioned earlier) to orchestrate and demonstrate the potential for a concerted, combined community public or private enterprise approach, on a massive scale, would offer some hope for the 1990s if the economic situation in the USA was not so bleak. Nevertheless by 1992 this foundation was working with over 200 non-profit housing groups in 90 cities. In Baltimore in a neighbourhood in which 44% of people seeking jobs are unemployed and which has one of the fifth highest crime rates in the US, their goal is to work with residents to transform all aspects of community life within five years. (Statement by J W Rouse to the Senate Committee on Banking, Housing and Urban Affairs, May 14, 1992).

The American version of squatting was also an effective vehicle for change. Cleverly dubbed 'Urban Home-Steading' to give the legitimacy of pioneer days, an early manifestation took place in Philadelphia in the mid-1970s where many abandoned buildings were owned by the Department of Housing and Urban Development. Public reaction largely supported the squatters. As similar actions were initiated in various cities, an Association of Community Organisations for Reform Now (ACORN) was formed. By 1980 ACORN was active in 36 states (Twelvetrees, 1989). Gradually desperation over the combination of homelessness and housing abandonment resulted in efforts in many cities to take over and make a case for legal assumption of empty houses (Borgos

1986, pp.409-10). Squatting became a tactic rather than an end. The aim was to build pressure for federal recognition of the need for government to address the housing needs of low and moderate income Americans. This culminated in the establishment of a 'Tent City' adjacent to the White House. In 1983 the Housing and Urban Recovery Act incorporated elements of the ACORN proposals on home-steading.

However by the end of the 1980s the number of homeless people in the United States was rapidly approaching the three million mark. The major federal response, the McKinney Act, which has encouraged research and demonstration projects, is primarily residual in its focus. The danger is that homelessness is defined as a private problem. As Ann Hartman pleaded in her editorial for an issue of the *Social Work Journal* (November 1989, p.483) devoted entirely to homelessness: the problem of homelessness is a public issue and can only be resolved through public action and major changes in public policy.

To this end the National Association of Social Workers adopted homelessness as its public service campaign for 1989 and in 1990, as previously noted, new Housing and Low Income Finance Acts became law. There are indications that President Clinton will make housing a high priority.

Conclusions

Where does this leave community work in the United States in the 1990s? What are the implications for activists in the United Kingdom? One effect of the Reagan/Bush years has been a deliberate refocusing on state and county responsibility for developing projects, initially in line with priorities set in central government but increasingly according to locally established needs and priorities. Meyer and Krauschaar note that the fifty states "have replaced the Federal Government as the major source of new initiatives for economic development" (*CDJ*, April 1989, p.96). Checkoway verified that there was more activity at the community level by the end of the eighties than in the sixties. More community workers were employed. Radicalism in terms of party politics may not have been evident but 'radical localists' as Checkoway termed them, certainly abounded.

What is perhaps most significant is that the scope of work and breadth of strategies have expanded. There is much greater emphasis on macro-structural analysis and political education, in creative tension with the local cultural context, which is still the fundamental organisational and development base. Though still locally rooted, the importance of developing links between organising efforts in diverse sites and contexts is recognised. There is also a greater appreciation of the importance of process, with a stress on the need for a clear value base rather than an ideological base. Reflecting on the first forty years of Alinsky type organising, the executive director of IAF commented (Boyte 1989, p.91):

> we were very good at the action, very clear and imaginative, but we didn't make a commitment to the growth process of the people. We never forced people to reflect.

In the UK I would suggest we all too often lacked a vision for concrete changes yet with the rise of community as a unit of practice, a community orientation pervades many more fields. This has its problems. Community is a slippery concept. It can and is applied as an attractive whitewash. Nevertheless, while this certainly complicates the picture for community workers, it also has the potential to expand and enrich the concept of community and democracy. By making it harder to package community work in one politically correct box, it could keep practitioners alert and open to various possible windows of opportunity. Davis considers this to be:

> a more exciting era than twenty years ago . . . not only related to the particular evolution of theory and practice in the United States, but also to the process by which international issues have become local issues. (Davis 1989, p.80)

All this should surely be heartening to community activists. We need to take risks, to embrace the complexities and the contradictions rather than search for certainty before we act. We need to vigourously take advantage of any windows of opportunity provided by the Right's professed rediscovery of community. Working from the community not only means that a groundswell of support can gradually be generated but programme ideas developed locally evolve as they are shared in other areas, allowing for essential refinement. There is also more opportunity for creative approaches to be discovered that reflect cultural diversity and minority values.

But is this enough? Can acting locally really have global impact? On the one hand, as far as economic change is concerned, the poverty statistics from the US are far from encouraging. Nevertheless there are remarkable examples of grassroots, comprehensive economic development. Politically the situation is volatile and wide open. "After the political parties break up" headlined *The Independent* re the USA (17.6.92). Evans and Boyte (1986, p.66) suggested that in the States the intimations of the beginning of a democratic populist movement were there in the Civil Rights Movement in the late sixties. While they saw signs of a populist movement that differed from the normal voting patterns, no stable political organisation developed. Perhaps it was too much to expect at that time; perhaps that is not the way for transformation. The challenge nevertheless is to coalesce the diversity of discourses in order to create sufficient momentum for the realisation of change instead of stalemate. Has the fallout from Reaganomics plus the arousal of middle America, the activity of new immigrants, the rage of the black and white underclass alongside the creative ongoing work of women now embracing diversity as they organise locally and network nationally, created a new dynamic? As people try, on the one hand, to realise the American dream and assert their right to be taken into account on their own terms and, on the other hand, to cope with life under the safety net, new alignments could result. A Canadian commentator predicted back in 1984 that

> society is ready for a new era of social change. And that change would involve a radical social transformation of the economic system . . . a more responsible human, consensual economy. (Blais 1984, p.26)

Wishful thinking or prophetic prediction? It is still not clear. James W Rouse in his statement to the US Senate (May 14, 1992) said that a true force for transformation stands ready to be unleashed through the thousands of neighbourhood non-profit development corporations in existence today (p.8).

However, one cannot simply combine groups (or countries) or mould movements that developed around specific issues into a new organ for comprehensive social, economic and political change, as Jesse Jackson found with his Rainbow Coalition. Reactionary forces also remain quite vigourous. The key, I suspect, is to focus on the process of organising rather than defining a banner under which to rally. The sort of mould-breaking change envisioned will likely erupt unexpectedly, suddenly coalescing the myriad of locally nurtured forces for change as in Montgomery, Alabama in 1955 or in Timisoara in 1989. The hope surely is that we can move beyond the traditional dichotomies for:

> we are so indoctrinated by our right/wrong, win/lose habits that we keep putting all our half-truths into two piles — Marxism versus Capitalism, science versus religion, economics versus social welfare, business versus labour and so on. We should seek rather a dynamic tension, a framework not a rigid structure, unity within diversity. (Ferguson 1980, p.229)

Revitalised and expanded mediating institutions or "free spaces", combined with the stress on process (collective action and reflection), on locally based development strategies combined with coalition building; could be the beginning. Perhaps we should celebrate the fact that community cuts across established ideologies, that it is indeed the site of intersecting discourses. Then people might be able to break out of their bipolarism and begin to create new alignments that would lead to the transformation of society.

Certainly this would seem to be the challenge and perhaps the heady possibility as we work towards the twenty-first century. Community workers actually know a lot about the features and factors necessary for this sort of organising. If we have learned anything from the last three decades it should be that it is the community which is the crucible for transformative, democratic change. For it is there that the intersection of the personal with the political is made possible.

References

Adams, M.L. (1989) 'There's No Place Like Home: On the place of Identity in Feminist Politics' in *Feminist Review*, No.31.

Alinski, *Saul Rules for Radicals.* (1972) and *Reveille for Radicals* (1969). Vintage Books.

Bell, D. & Tepperman, L. (1979) The Roots of Disunity, McCelland & Stewart Ltd.

Blais, R. (1984) 'Social Development Institutional Responsibility', p.26 in Issues in Canadian Social Policy, Vol.II.

Borgos, S. (1986) 'Low Income Homeownership and the ACORN Squatters Campaign' in Critical Perspectives in Housing, eds. Bratt, R.G. *et al*, Temple University Press.

Boyte, H.C. (1989) CommonWealth: A Return to Citizen Politics, The Free Press, Macmillan Inc.

Brager, G. & Specht, H. (1973). Community Organizing, Columbia University Press.

Burghardt, S. & Fabricant, M. (1987). Working Under the Safety Net Sage Publications, Human Services Guide 47.

Cawson, A. (1982). Corporation and Welfare, Heineman Educational Books, London.

Checkoway, B. (1985). 'Revitalizing an Urban Neighborhood: a St. Louis case study' in The Metropolitan Midwest ed. Checkoway & Patton, University of Ilinois Press.

Cox, F. & Garvin, C. (1987) in 'Strategies of Community Organization' F.E., Peacock Inc. (4th edition is now available, 1987).

Dalton, R.J. (1987). Citizen Politics in Western Democracies, Chatham House Inc.

Davis, A. (1989). 'Complexity, Activism, Optimism' in Feminist Review, No.31.

Doern, B. & Phidd, R. (1984). Canadian Public Policy: Ideas, Structures, Process Methuen.

Evans, S.M. & Boyte, H.C. (1986). Free Spaces: the sources of democratic change in America, Harper and Row.

Farley, R. (1984). Blacks and Whites: narrowing the gap? Harvard University Press.

Feit, R. & Peterson, J. (1980). 'Neighbourhood Women Look at Housing' in The Unsheltered Woman: Women and Housing in the 1980s, Centre for Urban Policy Research, New Brunswick.

Ferguson, M. (1980). The Aquarian Conspiracy, Tacher Inc.

Freire, P. (1972). Pedagogy of the Oppressed, Penguin.

Grant, J. (1988). Sisters Across the Atlantic, National Council for Voluntary Organisations.

Grossner, C.F. (1976). New Directions in Community Organisation, Preager Publishers.

Hall, S. & Jacques, M. eds. (1989). New Times, Lawrence and Wishart.

Hartman, A. (1989). 'Homelessness: Public Issues Private Troubles' in Social Work, National Association of Social Workers, Vol.34.

Hopps, J.G. (1988). 'Deja Vu or New View?' editorial in Social Work, National Association of Social Workers, Vol.33.3.

King, C.S. (1984). The Words of Martin Luther King, Collins. Kramer, R.M. & Specht, H. (1983). Readings in Community Organisation and Practice, Prentice Hall.

Kraushear, R. & Schmidt de Torres, B. (1982). 'The transformation of community work in the United States' in Community Work and the State, Craig *et al* eds., Routledge & Paul.

Nes, J.A. & Iadicola, P. (1987). 'Towards a Definition of Feminist Social Work' in Social Work, National Association of Social Workers, USA, Vol.34, No.1.

Ng, R., Walker, G. & Muller, J. (eds) (1990). Community Organisation and the Canadian State, Garamond Press, Toronto.

Perception, Vol.9, No.5, Canadian Council for Social Development, Ottawa — Summer 1989, p.14-5.

Pinkney, A. (1982). The Myth of Black Progress, Cambridge University Press.

Sayer, J. (1986). 'Ideology: The Bridge between Theory and Practice' in Community Development Journal, Oxford University Press, Vol.21, No.4.

Twelvetrees, A. (1989). Organising for Neighbourhood Development. Avebury, Gower Publishing Co. Ltd.

Wetherly, P. (1989). 'Class struggle and the welfare state' in Critical Social Policy, Issue 22.

Footnotes

1. See, for example, *New Times* (1989) eds. Hall, Jacques and Wetherly in *CSP* No.22 (p.39).
2. See, for example, Bell and Tepperman (1979), p.47.
3. See also Election Report, 1988, *The Sunday Times Magazine*: 'Land of the Rising Sons'.
4. See Andrew Brown's article "The Pilgrim's Progress" on the role of the Catholic Church in the crushing of Communism (*The Independent Magazine* 16.12.89).
5. For a thorough discussion of CDCs and Community Action Organisations see Twelvetrees 1989.
6. Conversations with Professor Barry Checkoway, University of Michigan, School of Social Work, 1987 and 1989
7. See for example Kraushar and Schmidt de Torres in Ch.13, p.144, Craig *et al,* (1982).
8. See the Institute for the Study of Drug Dependencey's 1989 study on Crack.
9. See for example Mary Louise Adams' article in *Feminist Review* No.31 (Spring 1989) on Identity Politics.
10. See Jane Grant's report to NCVO for a useful review of these organisations.
11. It is illustrative that in 1990 President Bush was willing to veto a Bill guaranteeing basic maternal leave rights.
12. The stock of public housing in the US has never been more than 2 percent.

11

Should Tenants Take Over?

Radical Community Work, Tenants Organisations, and the Future of Public Housing

Martin Wood

Introduction

Community workers, drawn from what Paul Waddington has described as the stable of 'radical dissenters', largely agree on the relevance of struggle in the area of the reproduction of labour (Waddington, 1983, p.41). Its constituent members have emerged from diverse sources but have in particular drawn upon and often combined neo-marxist, anarchist and feminist thinking. In contrast with the traditional left, who have largely restricted analysis and action to the work place, housing in general, and issues of concern to tenants in council housing in particular, are perceived by community workers to be an appropriate area of engagement.

This chapter examines recent developments in the provision and consumption of public housing and charts the response of tenants' organisations. Particular attention is paid to the campaign against the 1988 Housing Act and the subsequent development of tenant take-overs and tenant management initiatives. It further addresses the ideological dilemmas this has posed for radical community workers and activists in the tenants' movement alike. It seeks to clarify the issues and tentatively proposes a way forward.

From Attack to Defence

It is common now to identify a watershed period around the mid to late seventies and to draw a distinction between the activities of urban protest movements in Britain before this period and after it. Before this period locality-based tenants associations on council estates were predominantly engaged in volatile attacks against local authority housing departments. The condition of the stock, the repairs service and the bureaucratic, often patronising approach of housing officers and council members were all targets of their ferocity. City wide and occasionally national campaigns were mounted, rent strikes over issues such as rent rises, dampness, repairs and heating were common. Little attention or concern, if any, was paid to the political make-up of the local administration.

In contrast, during the subsequent period, from around about 1976 onwards up to and including present times, the activities of local groups has become increasingly aimed at defending rather than attacking the public sector and supporting rather than criticising local authorities in their struggle to maintain their stock. On a national level this defensive action included: campaigns against the cuts in central government housing expenditure, some opposition to the 'right to buy' provision of the 1980 Housing Act, and major campaigns against the voluntary disposal of council stock and the 1988 Housing Act. Opposition to the introduction of Housing Action Trusts and the so-called 'Tenants Choice' provisions of the 1988 Act were arguably the most strident examples of tenants' campaigns in recent times.

Community workers, in one guise or another, have been involved in these initiatives throughout and were often instrumental in the formation of tenants associations and federations. Many of the parochial struggles which characterised the early period were stimulated by innovative experiments in community work and, as Jerry Smith has noted, community work has helped to sustain an organisational base upon which the sporadic national campaigns could be built (Smith, 1992).

If the supportive role has remained the same, however, the attitude and approach of radical community workers has changed. The first period was characterised by optimism and plans for building alternative structures and a political movement while the latter was, and still is, a period of despondency and confusion. For some workers, the author included, this defensive period has constituted their formative years. It has not been an easy task for workers weaned on the conclusions of the Community Development Projects and inspired by their elders to explore the work of Gramsci, Castells and Freire, to reconcile their theoretical perspective with their experience on the ground.

Their first cause for concern was that traditional community action was no longer making the gains that it apparently used to. There continued to be minor coups — the provision of play areas and environmental improvements, the odd flower bed etc., but substantial gains — major refurbishment or re-development, for example — were few and far between. Groups have collapsed and workers and activists have found it increasingly difficult to respond to those who claim that group action makes no difference. The over-riding feeling was that increased centralisation of fiscal control had made the local administration an inappropriate or at least unfruitful target.

This did not constitute an immediate dilemma for those who perceived their task as encouraging critical reflection with a view to what Freire terms a process of 'conscientisation', since increased central control presented itself as an issue to be critically assessed (Freire, 1972). It did mean, however, that workers became increasingly concerned with the maintenance of the group rather than with their political awareness. Consequently, small gains secured through community action assumed inappropriate importance to both activists and workers simply because they re-affirmed the relevance of their activities in a hostile environment.

Secondly, whilst the message of the seventies had been about the importance of building regional links between groups in order to prevent authorities from playing one group off against another and national links to facilitate a relationship with wider labour, trade union and new social movements, the experience of the early eighties, with only a few exceptions, was one of reluctant parochialism. Community groups were forced, for example, into competing over scarce resources and over a limited flexibility in the allocation of local authority budgets. Furthermore, tenants' associations were increasingly being co-opted by local authorities or nullified by spurious consultation forums. Some degenerated into ameliatory social organisations, shunning political activity and others were taken over by political parties. The centre parties of the eighties continued the Liberal tradition of using community groups to make inroads into Labour strongholds but Labour activists have also from time to time swamped tenants associations, in order to offset criticism of electoral damage limitation exercises.

The 1988 Housing Act
In this light the national campaign over the 1988 Housing Act, despite its defensive nature, was a welcome relief and seemed to boost morale.

The intention of the 1988 Act was to:
- deregulate the private sector by introducing assured and assured shorthold tenancies with market as opposed to fair rents and a reduction in the security of tenure;
- cut the rate of government subsidy to housing associations, making them more reliant upon the vagaries of private finance and force associations to adopt assured tenancies, as above;
- impose an unelected and unaccountable board called a Housing

Action Trust (HAT) as landlord in the place of the local authority in specified areas designated by the Secretary of State;

● force local authorities to dispose of stock to private landlords or housing associations (where no more than 50% of tenants were against the transfer) through their spuriously titled 'tenants' choice' scheme.

These measures were clearly intended to continue the rundown of public housing which began in the early eighties. The Housing Investment Programme allocation, that is the amount of borrowing for major improvements and new developments permitted by central government, was halved between 1980 and 1984 and vast portions of the best stock were bought up by tenants under the 'right to buy' legislation. Since the voluntary transfer of estates, normally to housing associations, made possible in the 1985 Housing Act had, with few exceptions, failed to transpire, the government now seemed set on forcing the issue. Some local authorities began investigating the transfer option following the publication of the government's white paper in the autumn of 1988.

The National Campaign
The anti-sales campaign was underway before the Bill itself was published. National pressure groups, including Shelter and SCAT (Services to Community Action and Trade Unions) and the Labour Party were surprisingly quick off the mark picking up on the implications from the White Paper. Remarkably, housing officers who had traditionally avoided outspoken community activists, now fed them information and encouraged them to organise in opposition to the legislation. Many areas saw joint public sector trade union and tenant association action for the first time.

The news from community workers throughout the country was the same — a massive growth in local Tenants' Associations, the establishment of new federations, exceptionally large turn-outs at public meetings, unprecedented marches on town halls, ubiquitous "This estate is not for sale" posters and leaflets etc. A national network emerged rapidly. Facilitated by CASE (The National Campaign Against the Sale of Estates) and SCAT, trade unions came together with a plethora of federations drawn from various parts of the country. A new national federation was spawned. National conferences were organised by CASE, and the embryonic federation held a number of tenants only 'think tanks'. There were detailed workshops on: the implications of the legislation, opposing voluntary transfers and HATs, taking direct action, joint tenant and union action etc. and plans were hatched to mobilise a tenants' equivalent to 'flying pickets' with the intention of seeing off prospective landlords (*Community Action* No.80 and No.81). Thousands of tenants attended a national rally in Westminster Central Hall during the Lords stage of the Bill and two significant changes were forced. The Bill was amended to ensure that HATs could only be imposed where a majority of the tenants agreed, and the ballot procedures for the 'tenants choice' provision were changed to include a 50% turn-out requirement. The undemocratic voting procedure in which an abstention counted as a vote for the prospective landlord, however, has remained.

The campaign against HATs, voluntary transfers and the sale of estates was notably successful in the immediate aftermath of the Act. Not one of the nine originally designated HATs gained majority support from tenants and, by 1989, only two local authorities had successfully sold off large portions of their stock.

The picture has become increasingly blurred, however, as local authorities have investigated and negotiated more palatable deals with the Department of the Environment. In particular the appearance of the so-called 'voluntary' HAT has caused confusion. In 1991, just as housing campaigners were writing off the trusts, two local authorities — ironically both Labour controlled, were hatching plans for their revival. Substantial sums of money were made available and the government seemed prepared to bend the original idea significantly in order to see a HAT established. Hull and Waltham Forest saw the opportunity and successfully obtained significant concessions which include:

- an assurance that the local authority would be allowed to re-purchase property at the end of the HAT provided the tenant agrees;
- the freezing of rents during the period of the HAT;
- guarantees that all HAT properties would be available for rent;
- significant tenant representation on the board.

  (See Dwelly, 1991 and Owens, 1992)

Not surprisingly, given the extent of the investment — approximately £50 million in Hull and £170 million in Waltham Forest, tenants in these areas have welcomed the proposals and the ballot results have been impressive.

Whilst most commentators recognise the creative pragmatism of these authorities in securing this level of investment, Hull in particular has come in for criticism. The relatively tolerable condition of the property has caused concern as has their glitzy pseudo consultation process. Most significantly they have been accused of 'rail roading' tenants into an early ballot (Dwelly, 1991). Although Waltham Forest has been more cautious it is difficult not to agree with those who claim that their collusion has enabled the government to save face and has legitimised a ludicrous lottery where 'playing the game' secures the lion's share of the limited funds available. Other HATs are being explored in Liverpool and in Tower Hamlets (where one of the original HATs was rejected by tenants) but it is unlikely that they will be established anywhere else.

So far as 'tenants' choice' is concerned, the combination of a slump in the housing and development market and a high profile anti-sales campaign has effectively destroyed the threat of privatisation through this route at least for the time being. Interest in voluntary transfers on the other hand has experienced a significant revival. In the shadow of the Conservative's fourth consecutive electoral victory, for example, it was widely claimed that a hundred and fifty local authorities were investigating the large scale transfer of their stock.

The Role of Radical Community Workers

On the whole radical community workers drifted into supporting the anti-sales campaign, enthused by the massive mobilisation of angry tenants and committed to what many saw as a defence of socialist housing. Others were keen to support groups but anxious about the apparently uncritical attitudes of activists towards public landlords; the very authorities which they had previously criticised for being both bureaucratic and authoritarian.

To its credit, the campaign resurrected action aimed at securing a new tenants' charter. This would, it was hoped, include provisions for:

- the right to a warm dry house in a reasonable state of repair at an affordable rent;
- homes for persons with special needs;
- tenants consultation regarding the rent;
- security of tenure;
- tenants input in consultation.

(*Community Action* No.81)

The most celebrated campaign against the sale of estates took a very different slant. The Walterton and Elgin Action Group in Westminster engaged in a series of imaginative direct action raids on prospective developers. The action group bombarded the six companies involved with letters and phone calls and when they did not respond they sent a coachload of tenants armed with placards, posters, leaflets, songs and musicians and cameras to visit them. They invaded the offices and demanded that they withdrew from the scheme. Remarkably the group succeeded in knocking out all six of the developers (SCAT, 1989: WEAG, 1988).

Ironically, this group then proceeded to use the 'tenants' choice' provisions of the 1988 Act to turn the tables on their Conservative led council. They registered as a housing association, gained approved landlord status and took over their homes. These steps were taken reluctantly, however, as Jonathan Rosenberg, Community Housing Worker and co-ordinator of the group, explains:

> We've tried to create the next best thing to council housing. It's not better — no way. It doesn't have the capability to house as many people as should be housed and it never will. We've tried to make sure that it's even more democratic than council housing, but I still believe — and I think most people on the estates believe — that council housing is right and proper and that's how people should be housed. It's accountable, it's effective and it's fair. (Wech, 1992)

A similar message has come from tenants in Torbay, Devon, where the council had attempted, unsuccessfully, to transfer all of its stock to a housing association. Community workers employed by the Housing Advisory Bureau, set up by housing activist, Mike Drake, encouraged local tenants to organise themselves into associations with a district-wide federation. The federation has formed the Torbay Tenants' Housing Association with a view to taking over the stock.

Although these initiatives have not incurred the wrath of the tenants' movement and whilst, certainly in the case of the Westminster example, it has gained their support, 'tenant take-over' strategies are seen as a last resort rather than a positive alternative.

Little dialogue has taken place on the appalling record of some local authorities. Those who raised the idea of alternatives such as tenant management options at national meetings were shouted down by the leaders of the large federations who saw them as privatisation by the back door. In contrast radical community workers, whilst supporting the broad aims of the campaign, wanted to encourage a critical analysis of council housing. If council tenants were experiencing oppression in the sense of objectification in this form of tenure then this should be presented for analysis and action. The participatory as opposed to representative nature of democracy within housing co-ops, for example, was attractive and seemed to offer a potentially important alternative.

Co-operative Housing

Housing Co-ops both within and outside public housing increased in numbers significantly in the seventies and early eighties. Their emergence owed much to community action and alternative

perspectives of one form or another. Colin Ward has noted how in
some cases the establishment of a housing co-op merely amounted
to the legitimising of squatting (Ward, 1983, p.195). The history of
Stephen and Matilda Co-op in Wapping, the first tenant management
co-op in the country, is one of struggle and frustration. After four
years of campaigning and negotiation they eventually forced the
Greater London Council to agree to their demands. Although some
Labour authorities, notably Glasgow, Rochdale and Islington, have
actively pursued the development of management co-ops these
were the exception rather than the rule (NFHC).

Women's groups have a long history of campaigning for
co-operative housing. The Women's League and the Co-operative
Guild had argued for the Owenite idea of 'associated homes' with
communal facilities in the early nineteen hundreds (Yeo, 1988) and
these ideas have been echoed more recently by feminist community
workers:

> We fight for more and better public housing, but how often do we
> question the basic design . . . There is no room for the extended family:
> no room for groups of people living together; no concept of living units
> where some space is communal and some private . . . by giving people
> an increased element of control over their lives, co-ops can rescue this
> situation, for some. (Dixon *et al*, 1982)

Black groups too, like the black Roof Housing Co-op in Lambeth,
have also been attracted to the idea in an attempt to counteract and
by-pass institutional racism and the discriminatory practices of local
authorities (Roof, Nov/Dec 1986, p.19).

The upsurge in interest in the co-operative approach which
followed the implementation of the 1988 Act, however, had a very
different source. It was local authorities who were suddenly
promoting participation schemes and tenant management options.
Initially, it would appear, they simply wished to court tenants who
now had an opportunity to opt out, but more recently they have
been forced to pursue the development of Tenant Management
Co-ops or Estate Management Boards as a direct consequence of
Conservative Party policy.

Tenant Management Options

Tenant management co-operatives (TMCs) are, as the name
suggests, tenant controlled organisations which take on housing
management responsibilities. TCCs have corporate status through
registration with the Registrar of Friendly Societies and are therefore
in a position to negotiate a management agreement with their
landlord. Whilst the property continues to be owned by the council

and they normally maintain a responsibility for rent collection and major structural repairs, the co-op is able to take on the allocation of property, day to day and cyclical maintenance, environmental improvements and financial management. They are relatively autonomous and are normally managed through general meetings with a one member one vote system.

Estate management boards (EMBs) are similar. Tenants on an estate may become members of a registered association. Elected representatives from this association form a majority on a board which on the whole also includes local councillors and co-optees. Whereas TMCs are normally small and rarely manage more than a hundred properties, EMBs take on responsibility for the large estates. Although general meetings are held for members of the association, decisions are made by the board (see Power, 1991).

Central government has increasingly indicated that local authorities should move in this direction if they wished to gain its favour. The 1986 Housing and Planning Act compelled local authorities to consider proposals from tenants who wished to co-operatively manage their homes and Section 16 of the Act enabled the Department of the Environment to make grant payments to organisations supporting the establishment of tenant management options. More significantly tenant management, along with small scale disposal, was made an essential element in the granting of borrowing powers for Estate Action schemes and has become a significant element in the designation of City Challenge areas.

Those critical of the government argue that the motivation for these developments arose from a lull in 'right to buys'. Most of the viable sales had occurred and tenant management was perceived as an alternative step, if only a small one, in the direction of privatisation. Tenant co-ops were specifically mentioned in the 1988 Act as one of the bodies to which council housing could be transferred and the impression given by a recent promotional video produced by the Department of Environment is that they expect and wish to promote a linear progression from forming a tenants' association, to adopting a tenant management option, to opting out through Tenants Choice (DOE, 1992). That is, tenant management options are seen by them as the first rung on a ladder which leads to tenants opting out of local authority ownership all together.

Council members of all parties are understandably divided over the relative merits of tenant management options. Some enthusiasm has come from progressive, but not necessarily radical Labour groups, but the general consensus in town halls throughout the country is that there is no choice, either they play along or allow their stock to fall into an irreparable condition. Housing officers too commonly argue: 'We would have refurbished in the normal way, but now we have to impose tenant management options on tenants if we wish to carry out estate wide improvements'. Whilst they normally maintain that tenant involvement is a good thing in principle and consider it to be in line with a so called new 'customer orientated' approach their support is often half-hearted and owes more to the concepts of new wave management than to notions of collective empowerment.

New Financial Regime

Of course tenant activists see through this charade and glimpse the financial desperation which lies behind it. But if their analysis is sound, their prescriptions are scant. The movement as a whole holds a preference for the preservation of local authority provision, notwithstanding their demands for a more responsive service. They seem, however, to have their heads buried firmly in the sand. The 1989 Local Government and Housing Act, described by some as the 'death knell', slipped through parliament with little significant opposition from the tenants' movement. Under this piece of legislation: housing finance was ring fenced, rent subsidies from the rates/poll tax were halted and, since centrally financed subsidies were reduced to reflect the 'notional' as opposed to the actual expenditure from Housing Revenue Accounts, rent payers in council housing were left to pick up the rent rebate/housing benefit tab. When considered alongside the earlier restrictions placed on the spending of capital receipts from the sale of council homes it was clear that rents were set to rise and the quality of the stock was destined to fall (see Aughton & Malpass, 1990). It is worth noting that these developments should have been anticipated. Large scale unemployment has created a surplus labour force in Britain for over ten years and adequate housing, in the basic minimum sense, has therefore not been a necessary condition for the maintenance of capitalism during that time. Housing is always the first service to be cut in any slump and the recession of the early 1990s has been no exception.

The recent spate of interest in HATs and voluntary transfers must be seen as a direct consequence of this financial regime. Most of the latest attempts to transfer stock have been successful as tenants faced with unprecedented rent rises were effectively coerced into voting in its favour. Ironically the government has now moved to stem the flow, fearing the effects of large scale borrowing by housing associations and the implications that increased housing benefit payments would have on the public purse. The introduction

of compulsory competitive tendering for housing management in
1994/95, will further complicate the picture. Although councils will
continue to be responsible for policy decisions the housing service
itself will be put out to tender and provided by a contractor. Even
if the council's own housing department is awarded the contract
they will be required to operate separately.

The Way Forward
Radical community workers are faced with a difficult task. How can
or should they respond to these developments? Clearly workers
need to be realistic. Monolithic socio-economic structures are not
going to be significantly challenged in the short term but the
contradictions within these structures can be identified.
Fundamentally, workers should continue to promote dialogue and
critical analysis. It is only through this work that the dominant
capitalist ideology will be critically assessed and challenged.
Tenants' associations and the federation which hold together the
national movement should be encouraged to ask serious questions
and clarify their objectives. Does public housing in its present form,
with its implicit bureaucracy and paternalism, truly reflect their
hopes and aspirations? If not, can they subvert any of the alternatives
that are available in order to meet short term objectives —
maintaining high standards and affordable housing — and at the
same time experiment with structures which might in some way
fulfil some of their longer term goals and prefigure the kind of
provision they anticipate may result from wider structural change.
     Co-ops and tenant take-overs are important in this respect but
workers should encourage activists to be wary about their
imposition. Tenants' organisations need to take the high ground.
They should be offered the kind of information and support which
enables them to make their own assessment within a position of
confidence. All too often they are coerced into these schemes by
agencies who are paid to develop them and blamed by them when
they fall into difficulties. Those groups that pursue tenant
management and take over options will need to maintain links with
each other if they are not to be left isolated and increasingly
under-resourced. Whilst feminists and anarchists are right to
encourage experimentation with alternative organisational forms,
neo-marxists are also right to push for stronger links with a wider
political movement. It is not insignificant, for example, that as a
direct result of changes to Section 16 funding from the Department
of the Environment, which enables grant payments to be made to
organisations that promote and develop these schemes, that the

National Federation of Housing Co-ops, which linked disparate housing co-operatives, met its demise.

Where possible, radical community workers should encourage and support those who genuinely opt for alternative forms of management both inside and outside the state provision but they should be particularly careful to ensure that groups have the necessary support and the opportunity to build alliances with other co-ops and the tenants' movement as a whole. There will, almost inevitably, be hostility between these groups and traditional tenants organisations, but it is only through critical dialogue of this kind that a critical movement will emerge.

References

Aughton, H. & Malpass, P. (1990) *Housing Finance: A Basic Guide.* London: Shelter.

Dixon, G., Johnson, C., Leigh, S. & Turnbull, N. (1982) 'Feminist perspectives and practice' in Craig, G. et al (eds) *Community Work and the State.* London: Routledge.

DOE. (1992) "Tenants Extra: Tenant Participation in the Management of Council Housing". Department of the Environment.

Dwelly, T. (1991) "Too Much Trust" in *Roof,* March/April 1991.

Friere, P. (1972) *Pedagogy of the Oppressed* Harmondsworth: Penguin.

NFHC. *Tenant Management Co-ops — The Future.* London: National Federation of Housing Co-operatives.

Owens, R. (1992) "If The Hat Fits" in *Roof,* Jan/Feb 1992.

Power, A. (1991) *Housing Management: A Guide to Quality and Creativity.* London: Longman.

SCAT (1989) *We Are Not For Sale: Part Two.* Sheffield: SCAT Publications.

Smith, J. (1992) *Community Development and Tenant Action.* London: Community Development Foundation.

Waddington, P. (1983) "Looking Ahead — Community Work into the 1980s" in D.N. Thomas (ed) *Community Work in the Eighties* London: National Institute of Social Work.

Ward, C. (1983) *Housing: An Anarchist Approach* London: Freedom Press.

WEAG (1989) *Our Homes are Not For Sale* Video avaliable from Walterton and Elgin Community Homes Ltd., 204 Shirland Road, London W9 3JF.

Wech (1992) *Taking Over Our Homes* available from Waltreton and Elgin Community Homes Ltd., 204 Shirland Road, London W9 3JF.

Yeo, S. (ed) (1988) *New Views of Co-operation* London: Routledge.

12

Community Work in a Changing World

Sidney Jacobs

Radical Community Work in Thatcher's Britain
Community work in Britain developed during the late 1960s, at least in part, as a reaction against what was seen as the social control functions of both the welfare state and the state sponsored caring professions. Community work presented itself as a radical alternative to social work which it caricatured as "soft policing". Similarly, youth work was dismissed as a means of simply keeping working class kids off the streets. The welfare state, it was suggested, was designed to contain rather than cure poverty. For little more than a pittance, the poor were being bought off so as to avoid serious civil disorder. But, after 1979, the Thatcher Government, unleashing unbridled market forces, no longer considered that the cost of state welfare provisions was a price worth paying. As a consequence, millions of people found themselves unprotected and vulnerable, suffering long-term unemployment, homelessness and even hunger. Thus, in 1988/9, 12 million people were living below the poverty line compared to 5 million in 1979. During this period, the number of children in poverty rose to 3.2 million, an increase from 10% to 25% of all children in the country (*The Guardian*, 16 July 1992).

The Thatcher Government, rapidly abandoning the political consensus that had developed around social policy issues during the post-war years, proceeded almost immediately to dismantle the welfare state. Thus, community workers who had previously devoted their energies almost entirely to attacking the welfare state, now increasingly rallied to its defence. Marxists, in particular, while remaining highly critical of state welfare provision under capitalism, felt compelled to support it in preference to market provision. Thus, for example, the authors of the influential book, *In and Against the State*, urged socialists to defend working class living standards whilst undermining the state from within by building a 'culture of opposition'. The ultimate aim, it was stressed, was to pre-figure socialism whilst awaiting the anticipated overthrow of capitalism (L.E.W.R.G. 1980, p.132). It provided a rather neat formula allowing socialists to engage in so-called reformist activities while simultaneously retaining their supposed revolutionary purity. However, as a strategy, it worked in neither theory nor practice. By the end of the decade, it was, of course, communism not capitalism that collapsed. Now in the 1990s, the politics of insurrection, hardly still creditable, seemingly belong to a distant and quite different age. But, reformist strategies, designed to defend, let alone advance, the welfare state, clearly also failed during the Thatcher years. An early test was the 1980 Housing Act which allowed tenants to buy their council houses at bargain discount prices. Attempts to organise a mass campaign against sales were stillborn and deservedly so as it was largely imposed by outside activists rather than by council tenants themselves (see: Jacobs, 1981). Instead, by the 1990s, well over a million council houses were sold. The skilled working class, in particular, who had previously been deemed "deserving" and thus allocated the best and most saleable property, bought their council homes in their tens of thousands. In increasingly significant numbers, they also voted Conservative thereby endorsing the privatisation of the public utilities and the continuing erosion of the welfare state.

The early socialist response to Thatcherism was to demand the restoration of a reformed welfare state. It was to be based on principles of universalism, embracing both anti-sexism and anti-racism, plus a heavy dose of participatory democracy which of course, it never previously possessed. But, even these minimalist demands now seem wildly radical, beyond the realisms of practical politics. With the re-election of the Major government in 1992, the very foundations of the welfare state have already been seriously undermined and even its inner citadels, the NHS and state education, are in danger of crumbling. Indeed, if the welfare state survives at all, it is less likely to do so as a result of mass protest in the streets than from capitalism's inability to replace it with better and cheaper alternatives. As Offe (1982, p.11) predicted, the West cannot do without the welfare state for fear of 'exploding conflict and anarchy'. However, when he argues that the welfare state 'has become an irreversible structure', Offe seems to have misjudged the determination, no matter what the damage, of Britain's Right to privatise welfare. Clearly, much of the welfare state has already been reversed, albeit accompanied by growing street violence, lawlessness and sporadic urban rioting. In the processs, the very rich grew ever richer and the poor, poorer. Thus, for example, in 1988/9, tax cuts for individuals in the richest 1% of tax payers amounted to £22,680 per person, a sum greater than the total income of any single person in the bottom 95% of the population (quoted by Sivanandan, 1990, p.17).

Since 1979, the government has relentlessly cut public spending, intent on both residualising state welfare provision and centralising its administration. Within a climate of increasing authoritarianism, local government lost many of its decision-making powers. Thus, community campaigns, particularly those on purely local issues, became difficult to organise as protest needed more and more to be directed against Whitehall rather than City Hall. The power structure, in other words, became increasingly remote, unaccountable and unresponsive to popular pressure. Where previously Labour administrators or even "one nation" Tories, like Macmillan or Heath, could at times be moved by appealing to some supposedly shared notion of social justice, community activists soon learnt that the new occupants of Downing Street would not be shamed into making concessions to the poor. Their morality, being entirely derived from the ethics of the market place, can neither understand nor tolerate ideas of welfare collectivism. They apparently believe, as their Victorian predecessors did, in the "whip of starvation" to compel the "lower orders" to enter the "free" labour market. Increasingly intolerant of all opposition, the government remained stubbornly unreceptive to democratic demands from below, that is, until forced to reconsider by the overwhelming popular protest mobilised by the anti-Poll Tax campaigners.

Exposure to the cold winds of New Right extremism rendered radical community work increasingly isolated. The new wave of left Labour activists who swept to power in City Halls throughout much of urban Britain in the early 1980s, promised to transform Labour into a campaigning party, enhancing democracy through mass mobilisation at grassroots level. They spoke the language of radical community work which, however, mostly turned out to be mere rhetoric. But they did provide significant financial support for community projects which led to a brief flowering of innovative local activities, of feminist, black, gay, and a variety of other progressive causes, previously neglected by the funding agencies. But the money largely dried up when the Tories abolished the Greater London Council (GLC) and the Metropolitan authorities and generally drastically reduced the powers of local government. It seems that the Labour Left had neglected to even begin the process of building the masss movement they had promised and in the long term clearly failed to radicalise the Labour Party. As Ken Livingstone, former leader of the GLC candidly admitted;

we never really brought together the wider movement, or consulted them even . . . we slipped back into . . . fine speeches, heroic assaults and overlooked the fact the we didn't mobilize the community, we didn't mobilize the trade unions . . . (Livingstone & Campbell 1985, p.9).

Thus, when the Left ousted the old-style, right-wing Labour bosses from City Hall, the rhetoric changed but the rank and file remained as excluded from power and decision-making as they had always been. It is little wonder then that people did not take to the streets to defend the GLC and other so-called socialist local authorities. Still, their defeat left radical community work politically friendless.

As funds were continuously cut and political control tightened, community work learnt to operate with fewer resources and within less and less space than ever before. While still clinging to much of the radical rhetoric of the past, it has in practice now largely jettisoned whatever radicalism it once possessed. Thus, for example, community work students in Plymouth in 1992 produced a "value statement" as a guide to their practice which in its attack on inequality and injustice virtually promises to set the world alight. In reality, of course, it will do no such thing. Thus, the students are commendably urged to challenge discrimination, at both individual and institutional levels, on the basis of 'class, race, gender and sexuality'. It also commits them to:

. . . consciousness raising through educational and collective action . . . (and) a realisation of the structural inequalities within society and the need to work towards a redistribution of power and resources.

In other words, the values and aspirations of the next generation of community workers appear very similar to those which informed radical activists in the past. The problem, of course, is that the students are increasingly likely to find themselves on placement working to quite different agendas. In practice, the probability is that they will be unable, in any meaningful sense, to even question the "structural inequalities" existing within society. For that, it seems, is not what professional community work is really about these days. Clearly, community projects seeking to "redistribute power and resources", (to the working class, blacks, women, lesbians and gays?), are likely to be very rapidly closed down. After all, in a far more tolerant age, the Community Development Projects were disbanded in the 1970s essentially for arguing that it was structural inequalities inherent within capitalism, rather than the poor themselves, that were to blame for urban deprivation (see CDP, 1977). Moreover, most students nowadays actually seem to prefer working within agencies which are philosophically more at ease promoting "self-help" than "raising consciousness through collective action". Consensus rather than conflict orientated, their *modus operandi* appears more a matter of advocating on behalf of clients than helping local communities organise themselves for radical protest.

The focus of interest seems to have shifted away from the working class community to specific social problems such as drug addiction, alcoholism and AIDS. This is not in anyway to devalue this work (it desperately needs to be done) but merely to suggest that social workers and other specialists may be better qualified than community workers to undertake it. Community work seems generally to have retreated to the relative safety of youth work and the social services, that is, to the self-same welfare agencies it had previously so easily dismissed as reactionary. Some community workers, strangely oblivious to its ideological connotations, have quite effortlessly adopted the language of the market place, apparently comfortable in their new roles as "line managers" and "managers" no less. It is, of course, necessary to draw a sharp distinction between professional community work and community struggles which have continued unabated since 1979. It also needs to be stressed that individual community workers enthusiastically supported and often fully participated in these struggles, for example, the Miners' Support groups formed during the 1984/5 strike; the anti-Poll Tax campaign; council tenants against the 1988 Housing Act; and a variety of anti-racist struggles and countless other less well reported protests spread throughout the country. But, instead of gaining strength from the flurry of grassroots opposition to Thatcherite policies, community work seemed to feel itself threatened, turning its back on it as if the political ferment erupting all around had little or nothing to do with its new-found professional concerns. In the wake of the Miners' strike, community work, in common with much of the Left, seemed overcome with the paralysis of defeatism. The importance of linking struggles at the workplace with those in both the home and community, so powerfully demonstrated during the strike, has apparently been missed by mainstream community work. In short, community work's response to the misery of the Thatcher years recalls, perhaps unkindly, Miliband's (1973, p.108) damning assessment of the strategy adopted by Ramsey MacDonald's 1924 Labour government: 'having decided from the start that it would not do much and that it must not even try, it didn't'.

Community work has since 1979 been forced to operate under extremely difficult circumstances. Having now readily adapted to the demands of cost effective managerialism it has seemingly lost its radical edge. But, it needs to be understood, there never was a golden age of radical community work. Even during the 1960s and 1970s, its supposed heyday, it was, as its Marxist critics never tired of pointing out, mostly directionless and ideologically confused. Its lack of purpose during this period is brilliantly captured by Paris (1977, p.541): having reviewed three community work books and still remaining none the wiser about its aims and objectives, he evokes Matthew Arnold's vision of Dover Beach which, for its marvellous image of community work in blind confusion, is worth repeating here:

> And we are here as on a darkling plain
> swept with confused alarms of struggle and flight
> where ignorant armies clash by night

Community Work and Socialism

Although much of community work was a muddle, it did on occasions manage to organise working class communities, under their own leadership, in successful defences of their interests. What is more, many of these communities had previously been written off, by both the Right and the Left, as too apathetic, hopeless and unreliable, to do anything for themselves, let alone organise and sustain long-term campaigns. And, even though the sceptics scoffed, these struggles very often revealed, as the Bryants (1982, p.220) observe, genuine expressions of class consciousness. However, the gains made by community work during the 1970s were mostly small scale and short-lived. Further, during this period few if any advances were made in theoretical understanding. What socialists within community work simply offered was collectivist solutions to society's problems, attributed almost entirely to capitalism. That was accompanied by a passionately held but invariably ill-defined vision of an egalitarian future. Only the realisation of the "socialist project" held out the prospect of universal economic and social justice. Although woefully short on detail, it was this socialist vision which lifted radical community work out of the daily grind of bread and butter issues. It gave it, even if only in confused form, its ideological content, allowing activists to distinguish their politics from the bureaucratic, elitist Fabian traditions deeply embedded within the Labour Party. It was clearly important to distance community work from Fabianism which had always rejected the legitimacy of class struggle. For the Fabians, as explained by Hall & Schwarz (1985, p.23-4), 'the main agent of transformation would not be the masses but the agencies of the state itself'. Indeed, the aim of the Fabian Society, as recounted by Edward Pease (1916, p.255), its long serving secretary, 'has not been to make socialists, but to make socialism'. Thus, there were to be no socialists in the Fabian utopia. Community work aspires to stand Pease's vision on its head. As argued by Fleetwood & Lambert (1982, p.49), the business of radical community action must be, in the words of William Morris, 'the making of socialists'. In these terms, Left-wing activists in the early 1980s would have understood well enough what was meant by the editors of "Community Work and the State" when they declared their objective to be 'the development of a viable socialist practice' (Craig *et al* 1982, p.1). But, in the aftermath of the collapse of communism and the disintegration of the Soviet Union, Yugoslavia and much of Eastern Europe, we now need to know precisely what 'socialist practice' means. In the former communist states it signifies corruption, chaos and tyranny. In the West does it mean more than a social democratic or labourist accommodation with Capitalism?

Yet, there are still those who continue clinging to the old certainties, seemingly oblivious to the cataclysmic changes occurring in the world outside. As a consequence, community work's radicalism seems increasingly devoid of substance. Rarely if ever reflected in practice, it appears to serve no other purpose than that of allowing activists to define themselves in politically correct terms. But, it needs to be understood that it is both pointless and counter productive to continue blindly opposing capitalism when the socialist alternative to it no longer actually exists. Whatever our radical posturing, virtually no-one, even among Marxists, still believes in the efficacy of the Soviet-style command economy. On the other hand, the simple fact remains that it is in the very nature of markets to generate gross structural inequalities. We cannot, within the foreseeable future, hope to abolish the free flow of market forces but merely, to modify and ameliorate, as best we can, its worst effects. It is, of course, what the revisionists within the Labour Party have been preaching all along. But, in Mr Major's Britain of the 1990s even their limited vision seems to be rapidly receding as a practical possibility.

At the level of grassroots organisation it may seem that with the collapse of communism nothing much has changed. It is a far way from Britain's "Cardboard Cities" for the homeless or estates like London's Broadwater Farm, to Baku, Tbilisi or Sarajevo. For those struggling to survive in Britain on the margins of society, life must have seemed very much the same on the day after, as it was on the day before, the Berlin Wall came down. Moreover, as the origins of socialist inspired community work in Britain can be largely traced to the 1960s "New Left" revival which consistently opposed Soviet Communism, there is no reason whatsoever to now mourn its collapse. However, the problem is that it is not only Stalinism but also Leninism and the Bolshevik Revolution itself which have been discredited. And there is little evidence to suggest that Marxist economics actually work in practice. Further, in the past, particularly when attacking American Imperialism, even the most ardent anti-Stalinists seemingly felt compelled to find some good in the Soviet system. For example, Western Marxists commonly pointed to the apparent success of its social policies. These, it was said, compared favourably, not only with the squalor and mass poverty existing in the capitalist dominated Third World but also, in some respects with welfare provision in the West. Thus, attention was usually drawn to the attainment of virtual full employment, the large proportion of women in the labour force and to the relatively high standards achieved in health, education and child-care. This was all interpreted as the triumph of socialism even under Stalinism. At the very least, it was seen as evidence of socialism's potential to produce better things if only it could take hold in a mature industrialised society and thus be tried under more favourable conditions than those encountered by the Bolsheviks in Czarist Russia in 1917. Although not exactly providing a model for others to emulate, the Soviet Union at least hinted at the possibility of a socialist alternative to the welfare states provided under capitalism. However, it has become abundantly clear that the former Soviet Union failed miserably in every aspect of life: economically, politically and socially.

There is, in fact, nothing to be salvaged from the ruins of Soviet socialism. There are no redeeming features. Attempts by apologists to uncover any, miss the point that even in their most benign form, Kadorism in Hungary for instance, the essential nature of all the former communist regimes was their totalitarianism. The claims usually made in mitigation have little or no foundations. Thus, for instance, assertions that within the USSR poverty had been largely abolished have proved completely untrue. The alleged Western ills of corruption, crime, vice and prostitution, and much more besides, not only survived the overthrow of capitalism but continued to fester and flourish within the supposedly socialist countries. Far from fostering internationalism, as communist propaganda would have it, these were essentially sexist and intensely xenophobic societies. Certainly, the assumed strengths of Soviet social policy turned out to be much exaggerated if not entirely mythological. Moreover, it is perverse to measure the provision of creches and kindergartens on the same scale as mass murder, terror and labour camps. Under Communism, public transport was relatively cheap but then Mussolini was said, incorrectly as it turns out, to have made the trains run on time. To claim more for either system is to be deeply insulting to the memory of the millions of victims of both Stalinism and Italian Fascism.

In summary, it means that the socialist project no less, if not entirely illusionary has for the moment, at least, been severely stalled. A viable socialist blueprint for the future no longer exists, possibly not even in the faintest outline. It all needs to be urgently rethought. In terms of social policy, the Left seems to have run out of plausible ideas. The implication for community work is that, beyond tired well-worn Fabianism, there are neither long-term strategies nor visions on offer. In this context, its role during the 1990s is likely to be purely defensive.

Community Work and Class

It had long been confidently predicted by Western Marxists that eventually genuine socialism would be restored in the Soviet Union. Thus, according to Deutscher (1969, p.209) 'the democratic evolution of communism' would enable the working class to complete, or at least continue, the Bolsheviks' 'unfinished revolution' (Deutscher, 1967). He confidently expected that in due course the Soviet system would be transformed as a consequence of 'the full resurgence of the proletarian democratic traditions of communism' (Deutscher, 1969, p.209). The reality, of course, has turned out quite differently. While capitalism has been restored throughout Eastern Europe and the former Soviet Union, socialism is everywhere in retreat. Clearly, the working classes within those regions are, with good reason, disillusioned with communism. Far from re-discovering democratic socialism, they apparently prefer the extreme nationalism and racist intolerance peddled by the forces of right wing reaction. With the exception of the Czech Republic, there is little or no tradition of democracy in any of the former Soviet Bloc countries. In the West, on the other hand, the skilled working class have done reasonably well throughout the post-war years. For all its faults they have enjoyed the benefits of parliamentary democracy and, on the whole, rising living standards. Accordingly, the working class of the United States, Japan and Western Europe have shown little inclination to support revolutionary politics, leading in the early 1990s to the virtual extinction of Communist Parties in the West.

Eastern European intellectuals had long warned their Marxist counterparts in the West against romanticising labour. In particular, they argued that the orthodox Marxist belief in the existence of working class unity and hence, in the potential of class struggle to transform capitalism, was largely based on a myth. For example, as the Hungarian philosopher Vajda (1981, p.51) observed:

the proletariat as an integral class, undissolved into particular groups, has never existed under capitalism; nor has there been a demonstrable tendency pointing towards the development of such a class.

Whatever the historic truths of Vajda's observations, in Tory Britain of the 1990s, even within the context of deepening economic crisis, the prospect of a working class united in opposition to capitalism appears to be no more than an impossible and fast receding dream. Britain, in a period of rapid technological change was subjected to misguided monetarist policies, dogmatically adhered to, coupled with a ruthless political determination to tame the trade unions. During the early years of the Thatcher administration that led to dramatic de-industrialisation, restructuring and de-skilling and, through the rest of the decade, to persistently high levels of unemployment. Continuity in policy under Mr Major in the 1990s produced, for good measure, a second economic recession. In the process, the manual working class, Lenin's revolutionary vanguard, has been reduced to an ever declining minority within the population. Further, the deep divisions that had always existed within the class were continuously and deliberately widened by a ruling elite well practised in the political arts of divide and rule. Britain's so-called "aristocracy of labour" is overwhelmingly white, male, skilled and increasingly voted Tory. Although, historically, skilled workers have on occasions shown heroic self-sacrifice in the name of class unity, they have more often been inclined to protect their own sectional interests from competition from those below than act in solidarity with them. Indeed, an almost unbridgeable gulf appears to separate the top and bottom strata of the working class. There is very little that binds workers who have done reasonably well under the Tories with the millions in the so-called "new underclass" who have few prospects of permanently entering the labour market. Under those circumstances, for community work to simply appeal to "class solidarity" would seem to be singularly unhelpful. Community work needs to be highly sensitive to the differing interests, often conflicting but nonetheless legitimate which divide the various strata within the working class from each other.

In the above terms, community work strategy which is centrally informed by assumptions of working class unity appears mistaken in both theory and practice. In reality, working class neighbourhoods are typically poorly organised and riven by status, gender, "race" and ethnic divisions. In the early 1970s, community work's failure to win the unskilled working class for socialism convinced some activists to adopt a more directive approach to community work by assuming leadership roles within local organisations. The focus of attention was also shifted from "the poor" to the already politically conscious in the organised labour movement. In other words, campaigns were to be conducted on behalf of, rather than by, the poor. It was apparently to be done in the name of class solidarity. It constituted, in effect, a fairly crude and largely unsuccessful attempt, to apply Leninist vanguard theory to community work. Thus, Cockburn (1977, p.160) took community work to task for attempting to organise not the working class per se but the poorest sections of the population. Community work, she argued, only encouraged local groups to compete with one another for scarce resources thereby fostering "community" as opposed to "class consciousness". The implications are that activists unwittingly or otherwise, collude with the state to deflect workers from class struggle. But, as Smith (1981, p.57) observes, it taxes credulity to believe that 'community work is putting the lid on working class revolt'. In all this, it is suggested here, Cockburn could not have been more wrong. If community work has a role at all, it is primarily to help organise those at the bottom of society who, for reasons of unemployment, patriarchy, racism, old age and disability, fall outside of the protective umbrella of the labour movement. While the trade unions in particular hardly need help from community work, it is the poor, whose position is continuously deteriorating, who clearly constitute its natural constituency. Thus, for example, between 1979 and 1992, the value of unemployment benefit fell by about a third. In 1992, Britain had the lowest level of state benefits in the Western world. An average British family received a weekly payment of £105.29 in income support, mortgage interest repayment and poll tax relief. In comparison the level of benefit in France was £154.95; in the United States, £166; and in Spain £172. All other Western countries provided more than £200 per week, including £222 in Japan; £252 in Germany; and £346 in Sweden (quoted in *The Observer*, 16 August 1992).

Organising Among the Poor
The New Trade Unions of the 1880s which organised among semi-skilled workers, the National Unemployed Workers' Movement (N.U.W.M.) (active during the inter-war years) and the 1940s squatters movement are but three examples of the successful mobilisation of those near, or at the bottom of society. However, the British Labour movement has only exceptionally reached the poor and poorest within the population, traditionally having viewed

them with a mixture of compassion, contempt and mistrust. The tone was, of course, set by the "Communist Manifesto" which stereotypes those at the very bottom, "the lumpen-proletariat", as the 'dangerous class, the social scum, that passively rotting mass thrown off by the lowest layers of the old society . . .' (Marx and Engels, 1968 edition p44). During the late 19th century, the Social Democratic Federation (SDF), the forerunner of the British Communist Party, concentrated its propaganda, without much success, on the unemployed. Their failure is well illustrated by the events which occurred during the famous 1886 riots in Trafalgar Square. After a meeting for the unemployed organised by the SDF, the crowd 'smashed windows and looted Mayfair shops'. On their way back to the East End, they sang "Rule Britannia", which, as Stedman Jones (1971, p.345) notes, is 'an eloquent testimony to its confused and limited level of political consciousness'. Indeed, according to Hinton (1983, p.30) 'the great mass of urban poor', constituting about 40 per cent of the British working class in 1900, remained 'impermeable to working class organisation'. Hinton considers that the major obstacle to working class unity during this period was the labour movement's inability to organise among the poor in general and women in particular. With Britain then at the height her imperial strength, he could well have added racism to the list of hindrances to class unity. It seems that very little has changed. Now, at the end of the century, poverty, patriarchy and racism still remain the great unresolved issues of the age. Clearly, it is with these that community work needs to engage.

By focusing on their perceived common class interests, community work aims to transcend the status, gender, race and other divisions existing within working class communities. But these are volatile times and activists need to tread carefully for fear of exacerbating, rather than bridging, existing differences. With the re-emergence throughout Europe of extreme right-wing nationalism and organised neo-Nazi thuggery, racism must everywhere be opposed. Thus it is essential that "community" as an arena for struggle is not abandoned to the Right. However, there is little evidence to suggest that community struggle actually raises political consciousness. Even among the working class leaders that emerge during campaigns, few, if any, necessarily acquire a clear vision of an alternative social order. Indeed, there is some historical evidence which even suggests the opposite. Thus, Melling (1983, p.71) tells of an activist during the 1915 Glasgow Rent Strike who 'played a prominent role in mobilising local tenants' but who still 'remained a life-long Tory and Orange leader'. Similarly, one of the leaders of the Burston School Strike which lasted from 1914 until 1939, was 'an avowed Conservative' (Zamoyska 1985, p.55). Certainly, the Left should not assume that it has a monopoly within community politics. The record of socialism in practice, in the Soviet Union, Eastern Europe and China, on race, gender, nuclear weapons, ecology, indeed, on most of the issues of central concern to the "new social movements", has generally been quite appalling. Similarly, in the West, while the Left commonly claims these causes as its own, its practice is often racist, sexist, militaristic and ecologically unsound. While the need to build socialism from below remains as urgent as ever, the Left's attempts to do so, including community work's, have so far proved somewhat less than encouraging.

The Left, from Marxists to Fabians, while seeking social justice on behalf of the poor and poorest in society, invariably excludes them from power and decision-making. It appears that it was never intended that the foundation stones of socialism should be laid at the very bottom of society. Perhaps it is entirely unrealistic for community work to have ever expected otherwise. Certainly Marxist orthodoxy warns that the bottom strata is not to be trusted because, as expressed in "The Communist Manifesto", 'its condition of life prepares it for the part of a bribed tool of reactionary intrigue' (Marx & Engels, 1968, p.44). In Marxist terms, those who survive in abject poverty, largely outside of the formal economy will hardly share any common class interests even with the "reserve army" immediately above them let alone with organised labour. As colourfully described by Marx (1946 edition, p.659), 'the lowest sediment of the relative surplus-population finally dwells in the sphere of pauperism' which he calls, 'the hospital of the active labour-army and the dead weight of the industrial reserve-army'. Community work needs to approach organising among the so-called "lumpen proletariat" with considerable modesty and awareness of its own limitations. Unsuccessful interventions can, of course, do great harm, in particular to vulnerable communities.

White (1986), in his fascinating study of "Campbell Bunk — the worst street in North London" provides a wealth of material highly relevant to community work. For instance, he shows that in conditions of dire poverty and recurring male violence, the women there created mutual aid networks. Their concern was both with women's survival and the protection of children and young adults (p.75). Community workers will know from their own experience that, even in the most deprived and depressed areas, people will constantly demonstrate their seemingly endless capacity to help and care for one another. Despite these manifestations of self-help, communities at the very bottom of society, with limited or no experience of collective action, do not provide the most fertile ground for outside community work intervention. Not least of all because of the intense hostility usually felt towards strangers who rarely, if ever, venture into them. White shows that the people of Campbell Road developed a 'complex and contradictory' worldview which he identifies as 'egalitarianism', 'individualism', 'libertarianism' and 'chauvinism' (p.102). Largely parochial, these values in sum and separately would seem to be antipathetic to the growth of class consciousness and solidarity. Their common worldviews, White suggests, 'were inherently resistant to socialist propaganda; the reaction against discipline, anti-internationalism, and most of all, individualism' (p.108). Contrary to expectations, he did not find support for Mosley's fascists during the 1930s, which he explains by the strength of prevailing anti-German prejudice. Indeed, 'chauvinism', defined as 'an aggressive dislike of people (and things) who were not English' (p.102) was widespread and commonly expressed in both anti-Irish sentiment and anti-semitism. White (p.105) also recounts anecdotes of 'how black men were run out of Campbell Road in the 1930s after exemplary beatings from residents'. Thus, while any outside activist attempting to organise in the Campbell Bunk's of this world is likely, initially at least, to encounter considerable suspicion and hostility, even entering such places, it would seem, is dangerous for black community workers.

In areas of extreme poverty, where socialist and trade union traditions are weak, local community groups are bound to prove difficult to organise and, over any length of time, even harder to sustain. The poor have good reason to view representatives of the welfare state with deep suspicion, even when appearing in the apparently friendly guise of community worker. Experience will have taught that it is usually best to remain unknown to the power structure, avoiding whenever possible the potentially suffocating web of its bureaucratic embrace. Even during its supposedly benevolent pre-Thatcherite period, the welfare state consistently oppressed those who most depended upon it for their survival. In return for slum housing and income support which since 1979 is increasingly below subsistence level, the state demands constant deference, conformity and loss of dignity. In these terms attempts by community work to mediate between the state and the poorest sections of the population are based on a series of spurious assumptions, not least of all, that the powerful in society share common national interests with those at the bottom. It is essentially a consensual approach to community work, labelled 'social planning' by the Bryants (1982, p.211), which aims 'to produce a more sensitive and responsive fit between the policies of local government and the needs of local groups'. Although seeking, rhetorically at least, to act on behalf of the poor, invariably it comes to represent not their interests but those of the state. If needs be, it will even operate directly against rather than for the poor. At best, it is an approach that is capable of reaching only local "worthies" and the so-called "respectable" working class, usually at the expense and exclusion of those deemed "undeserving". Largely ignoring class and class conflict, it seeks to convince the main casualties of the market economy that the state under capitalism is essentially neutral rather than exploitative, patriarchal and racist. Clearly with the collapse of communism, capitalism has not suddenly become benign. On the contrary, with its ideological rival finally discredited, capitalism now has less reason than ever before to respond to pressure for social reforms coming from below. For the moment at least, social policy is no longer required to act as "an antidote to socialism".

While conventional community work may have little to offer the poor, more radical approaches would seem to be equally problematic. In Britain opposition remains extremely difficult against a largely intransigent government still retaining the siege mentality and paranoia it acquired during the Thatcher years. Far from being sympathetic to the plight of the poor, it is intent on making them pay for successive economic crises. Under these circumstances, direct confrontation, unless there is a good chance of winning, may seem unduly provocative, pointless and possibly even dangerous. The ruling class, it needs to be remembered, has always been especially vindictive towards the rebellious poor. In these terms, community campaigns, while possessing little chance of significantly altering the status quo, may simply serve to unnecessarily draw attention to the leading local activists, leaving them exposed to possible victimisation and harassment. Clearly, community workers need to be very sure of what they are doing before they begin, in the name of socialism, feminism or whatever, to intervene in the lives of people who because of their poverty are extremely vulnerable to retribution from authority.

The labour movement, traditionally representing the skilled working class and, increasingly now, white collar workers, marginalises the poor, mostly excluding them from its ranks. While generally better off under Labour than the Tories, the poor could be forgiven for feeling that Labour has promised much but has, over the years, delivered relatively little. Determined above all else to convince capitalism that they are "fit to govern", Labour's leaders, from Ramsay McDonald to Kinnock, have distanced themselves from the poor and in the process abandoned whatever lingering socialist vision they might have still possessed of an egalitarian future. Certainly Labour largely shares prevailing stereotypes about the alleged criminality, immorality, fecklessness and propensity to scrounge of the so-called "underclass". In practice, Labour is hardly much more tolerant than are the Tories of insubordination, real or imagined, emanating from below. Thus, while the poorest in society often possess an abysmally low level of political and class consciousness, this in itself does not fully explain their indifference, antipathy even, towards organised labour. That also needs to be seen as an expression of very real conflicting interests which divide the top and bottom structure of the working class. Thus, for example, White (1980 p108) notes that the residents of Campbell Road, on the fringes of the docks and building trades, opposed the basic trade union demand for "decasualisation" for fear that this would limit employment opportunities for those, like themselves, on the industrial margins. As White found, 'there was considerable hostility within Campbell Road to trade unions'. Thus when attempting to organise in such areas merely appealing to their sense of class solidarity is unlikely, initially at least, to prove very helpful.

Mann (1992, p.160) lists the wide variety of terms and concepts, mostly ill-defined and containing moralistic overtones, that are commonly used to describe the bottom layer of the class structure. He argues that there is a need to develop a new terminology which 'does not denigrate the poorest sections of the working class, recognises their combativity and acknowledges their vulnerability'. Indeed, community workers believing otherwise have no business intervening in poor working class areas. In other words, if community work is to offer more than old fashioned philanthropy, it needs to resolutely reject perceptions of the poor as passive victims, apathetic and incapable of organising even in their own interests. As an example of the 'poor forming their own defence organisations', Mann (1992, p.141) points to the N.U.W.M. which organised the unemployed through the inter-war years and whose very impressive record includes the mounting of several mass hunger marches. The N.U.W.M. was, of course, under communist leadership, which raises questions about the extent to which it was actually controlled by the unemployed themselves rather than the Communist Party. Indeed in many of the famous struggles of the past, the leadership was often provided by outsiders, often middle class. Space does not allow for further discussion here of this issue other than to note that the role of the intellectual in working class movements pre-occupied many of the early socialists. As the question remains critical for community work, as indeed it does for socialists everywhere, there are important lessons still to be learnt from the historical debates [See: Levy (1987)]. In the aftermath of Stalinism, it would seem almost self-evident that socialism needs to re-establish its democratic credentials. And that means, if democracy means anything at all, re-building the movement from below with the poor being in control of their own organisations.

The extent to which the N.U.W.M. succeeded in recruiting among the long-term unemployed, particularly the unskilled at the very bottom of society, also remains uncertain. Thus, Wal Hannington (1937, p.248), the N.U.W.M.'s chronicler and leading activist, regretted that 'the great mass of the unemployed remained unorganised'. Hannington goes on to observe:

> In spite of all that has been done, unemployment remains, widespread poverty exists, and the distressed areas have not been restored to life and prosperity. (p239).

Thus, where the N.U.W.M. failed, modern community work is most unlikely to succeed. However, there are those like Sivanandan (1990, p.28) who feel that in Britain in the 1990s it is only the "new underclass" who now have 'nothing to lose but their chains, nothing to choose but survival, and are therefore dynamic, open, organic'. As an example he points to the residents of Broadwater Farm estate in North London who, after racist policing and the disturbances there in 1985, 'came together to create a life for themselves'. He found that they:

> set up a nursery, provided meals and a meeting place for pensioners, established a centre for youth and built up, in the process, a political culture that resisted police intrusion . . . (p.25).

Davis (1989, p.79), however, doubts the existence on the Broadwater Estate, both before and after the riot, of a 'permanent community, with all its connotations of shared values and sentiments'.

It would seem that Sivanandan, by suggesting that the "new underclass" virtually constitutes a new revolutionary class, overstates his case. However, he does convincingly demonstrate that people, in areas like the Broadwater Farm Estate, when given the opportunity, are perfectly capable of organising themselves. Further, the process of building their own organisations invariably releases an enormous amount of creative energy, revealing a variety of talents and abilities. And this from people conventionally written off as too hopelessly demoralised and inadequate to do anything very much for themselves or anybody else. It is here, among the growing numbers of the dispossessed in Britain, now roughly one in three of the population, that community work needs to forge a role for itself in the 1990s. In other words, it needs to reaffirm its traditional beliefs in community struggle as an authentic expression of class struggle even if it is small-scale and limited in its wider political implications.

Although communism has collapsed, it needs to be understood, that class conflict continues unabated. Certainly, no-one appears to have informed Capitalism that the class war has ended. Capital, as ever, still continues in its relentless pursuit of profit, exploiting and oppressing the vast majority of the people of the world. The poor everywhere have, from their own bitter experiences, a profound understanding of capitalist exploitation. And that requires to be the starting point for community work intervention in working class areas. The exceptions, roughly conforming to Marxism's description of the "lumpen proletariat", do exist, as is illustrated in White's study of the Campbell Bunk. There is no doubt that modern equivalents not only survive but are also constantly being replenished in Britain in the 1990s, as growing unemployment, poverty and homelessness, together with cuts in welfare spending, take their toll. Still, all the indicators are that so-called "lumpen" elements constitute only a small minority of the population. Community workers seem to be particularly ill-equipped to deal with their problems, which are best referred to social workers and other professionals trained for the purpose. Instead, community work needs to concentrate its efforts on the vast majority of the poor who, in a wide variety of situations, have repeatedly demonstrated both their ability and willingness to organise themselves under their own leadership and, where necessary, to sustain long-term campaigning. Community work needs to engage, even if on a small scale in our own back yards, with the great political issues of the age — poverty, racism, patriarchy, the plight of refugees, the renewed danger of fascism and the impending ecological disaster which threatens to overwhelm us all.

References

Bryant, B. & Bryant, R. (1980) *Change and Conflict*, Aberdeen University Press.
Cockburn, C. (1977) *The Local State*, Pluto.
Community Development Project (1977) *Gilding the Ghetto*, CDP.
Craig, G., Derricourt, N. & Loney, M. (eds) (1982) *Community Work and the State*, Routledge.
Davis, J. (1989) From 'Rookeries' to 'Communities': Race, Poverty and Policing in London 1886-1985, *History Workshop* 27.
Deutscher, I. (1967) *The Unfinished Revolution: Russia 1917-1967*, Oxford University Press.
Deutscher, I. (1969) *Heretics and Renegades*, Cape.
Fleetwood, M. & Lambert J. (1982) 'Bringing Socialism Home: Theory and Practice for a Radical Community Action' in G. Craig *et al Community Work and the*

State, Routledge.

Hall, S & Schwarz, B. (1985) 'State and Society, 1880-1930' in M. Langan & B. Schwarz (eds.) *Crises in the British State 1880-1930*, Hutchinson.

Hannington, W. (1977) *Unemployed Struggles 1919-1936*, Lawrence & Wishart.

Hinton, J. (1983) *Labour and Socialism*, Wheatsheaf.

Jacobs, S. (1981) The Sale of Council Houses. Does it matter? *Critical Social Policy*, 1,2.

Levy, C. (1987) *Socialism and the Intelegensia 1880-1914*, Routledge.

Livingstone, K & Campbell, B (1985) Rate-capping and Re-alignment, *Marxism Today*, May 1985.

London Edinburgh Weekend Return Group (LEWRG) (1980) *In and Against the State*, Pluto.

Mann, K. (1992) *The Making of an English 'Underclass'?*, Open University Press

Marx, K. & Engles, F. (1968 edition) 'Manifesto of the Communist Party', in *Marx & Engles, Selected Works*, Lawrence & Wishart.

Marx, K. (1946 edition) *Capital*, Allen & Unwin.

Melling, J. (1983) *Rent Strikes*, Polygon.

Miliband, R. (1973) *Parliamentary Socialism*, Merlin.

Offe, C. (1982) Some contradictions of the Modern Welfare State, *Critical Social Policy* 2,2.

Paris, C. (1977) 'Where Ignorant Armies Clash by Night': The Community Action Movement, *International Journal of Urban Regional Research*, 1,3.

Pease, E. (1916) *The History of the Fabian Society*, Fifield.

Sivanandan, A. (1990) 'All that Melts into Air is Spoiled: the Hokum of New Times', *Race and Class, 31*, 3.

Smith, J. (1981) 'Possibilities for a Socialist Community Work Practice', in P. Henderson & D. N. Thomas *Readings in Community Action*, Allen Unwin.

Stedman, Jones, G. (1971) *Outcast London*, Penguin.

Vajda, M. (1981) *The State and Socialism*, Allison & Busby.

White, J. (1986) *The Worst Street in North London*, Routledge.

Zamoyska, B. (1985) 'The Burston Rebellion', Ariel.

Notes on Contributors

Jennifer Dale is a lecturer in Social Policy in the Department of Social Policy at the University of Manchester. She has a special interest in housing and has written about tenant participation, and feminism and social welfare.

Nick Derricourt worked as a community worker in the 1960s and early 1970s before becoming involved in training at Birmingham and Sunderland Polytechnics. Since 1978 he has taught in the Department of Social Administration (now Department of Applied Social Science) at the University of Lancaster, and has written mainly about community work, community social work, and community-based mediation schemes. He is especially interested in the problems of evaluating community work and of facilitating groups in community work.

Lena Dominelli is Professor of Social Administration at the University of Sheffield. She is a qualified social worker and has worked as a community worker, social worker, and probation officer. Her main interests are in the field of anti-oppressive social work and she has written extensively in this area. Her most recent books include: *Anti-Racist Social Work* (BASW/Macmillan 1988); *Feminist Social Work* (with E. McLeod) (Macmillan 1989); *Women and Community Action* (Venture Press, 1990); *Women across the Continents; Feminist Comparative Social Policy* (Harvester/Wheatsheaf. 1991); *Gender, Sex Offenders and Probation Practice* (Novata Press, 1991).

George Giacinto Giarchi is Head of the Community Research Centre at the University of Plymouth. Formerly a youth counsellor and social worker in Plymouth, he now lectures in Community Studies and in the Community Care of the Elderly in Rural Areas of Europe. He is an active researcher in comparative community case studies and author of *Between McAlpine and Polaris* (RKP 1984) and of numerous articles and research reports. He has two books forthcoming: *Sociology of Ageing* (Longmans) and *Elderly Care in Greater Europe* (Gower).

Bob Holman was an academic before spending the last sixteen years working in community projects. He is author of *Good Old George: The Life of George Lansbury* (Lion, 1990). He lives in Easterhouse, Glasgow.

Sidney Jacobs was a community worker in Glasgow and London during the 1970s before becoming Senior Lecturer in Social Administration at the University of Plymouth. In addition to Community Work, his research interests include Race, Housing and Labour History.

Ann Jeffries went to live in California as a young woman in 1960 and was politicized by the Civil Rights Movement. She worked for many years with women in public housing estates, initially in Michigan as an Outreach Social Worker employed by the Child and Family Services Agency and subsequently in Canada as co-ordinator of a child abuse prevention demonstration project. On returning to the UK in 1986 Ann took up a teaching post in the Department of Applied Social Science at the University of Plymouth where she is now a Principal Lecturer.

Keith Popple is a Senior Lecturer in Social Policy in the Department of Applied Social Science at the University of Plymouth. A qualified social worker, he worked as a youth worker and as community worker in the West Midlands before teaching at Westhill College, Birmingham and Sunderland Polytechnic. His main interests are in the field of youth policy and the theory and practice in community work. He was a founder editor of the journal *Youth and Policy.* He is co-editing with Jan Hazekamp a forthcoming book, *Racism in Europe: a challenge for youth policy and youth work* (UCL Press).

Viv Rogers was a community worker in Plymouth and now lives and works in Bristol.

Ranjit Sondhi was previously co-ordinator of the Asian Resource Centre, Handsworth, Birmingham. He is now Senior Lecturer in Youth and Community Work, Westhill College, Birmingham. He is also Chair, Refugee Education Training and Enterprise Forum, Voluntary Services Unit, Home Office; a member of the Radio Authority; Director of Birmingham Training and Enterprise Council and a Deputy Chair of the Commission for Racial Equality. He writes and lectures on black issues.

Paul Waddington was a town planner and has been employed variously since the late 1960s as a community worker, C.D.P. action-research worker, and teacher of community work and urban policy. He is now Professor of Applied Social Studies and Assistant Dean of the Faculty of Health and Social Sciences at the University of Central England in Birmingham. He is currently undertaking a research project on the community care planning process in selected Midland localities, on secondment to the Local Government Centre at the University of Warwick.

Haydae White is currently a part-time freelance trainer/consultant and a part-time play officer in Bristol. Aiming to promote race equality in practice, she has worked as a social worker, community development worker, student unit supervisor and social work lecturer.

Martin Wood studied Social Policy and Community Work at Plymouth Polytechnic (now the University of Plymouth) and at the Cranfield Institute and worked in the voluntary sector as a community development worker where he specialised in housing issues. He now works as a Training and Development Worker for a Tenant Participation agency in North East England and lectures on housing policy at the University of Teesside.